Y0-BZV-402

married baggage without

Interior Design: Dan Robinson
Cover Artist: Mark Stay
Cover Design: Charles Rivers, Dan Robinson
Printed in the USA.

ISBN 10: 09758984-4-2
ISBN 13: 978-09758984-4-4

PUBLISHING

married baggage without

How to Love One,
By Forgiving Many

CHARLES RIVERS

FILA
PUBLISHING

Additional Marriage Support Books by Charles Rivers

How to Get the Most In Marriage
How to Become your Spouse's Best Friend
The Good Marriage Maintenance Kit
Heart of the Marriage

CONTENTS

BOOK I —
UNCLAIMED BAGGAGE

BOOK 2 —
DOMESTIC BAGGAGE

Book 3 —
Baggage Handler

BOOK 4 —
SURRENDERED BAGGAGE

Acknowledgments

To all of those couples who were brave enough to allow me to make a difference in their marital life.

Thank you.

DISCLAIMER

Each couple's story in this book, although factual, is represented by a name change to allow them anonymity.

FORWARD

Too Much Emotional Baggage? Consider Unpacking

Do you remember the old question that they used to ask at the airport when you were checking in for your flight? Pre-9/11 the question was always; did you pack your own bags? Has anyone, but you handled your bags prior to arrival here? The correct answer to this question that they were looking for was yes; you packed your own bags. So let me ask you this, did you pack your emotional bags? Has anyone, but you handled your bags prior to getting to where you are right now in life?

If you can't answer yes to these questions, then it's time to pull open those emotional bags and sort them out. It could be that some resentments, fears and self-loathing have crept in when you weren't looking and for your emotional well being as well as the emotional well being of your relationship, it's time to unpack the bad from the good.

How to Unpack Emotional Baggage?

How you unpack your emotional baggage is going to be very individual to the person you are and the person you were. After all, our relationships often affect us in more ways than we can tabulate. If you had a relationship with someone that constantly competed with you, but it wasn't healthy competition — it was a competition that your partner had to win. Your partner had to be the best, they demanded it and in the process they made you question your own self-worth — chances are that's packed in your emotional baggage as well.

Maybe you had a relationship with someone that constantly compared your qualities to others and found you lacking. Male or female, this kind of constant comparison can damage your self-esteem and self-image and leave you feeling unattractive. Considering that many of us act the way we feel, we hoard this poor self-image in the bottom of our emotional baggage and sometimes, we forget that it's there.

So how do you unpack all of this emotional baggage and overcome the bad stuff? Take a lesson from childhood and play pretend. Seriously. We are how we feel. If we think we aren't beautiful or attractive, we stop acting that way. If we think we're not good at anything, we stop putting forth effort. So when you begin cleaning out your baggage, pack in there what you want to be in there — attractiveness — act attractive, believe you are attractive. Pack in confidence and self-worth — believe you can do anything if you just put forth the effort.

Pack your own bags — your past relationships should not discolor your present. There is a truism in the idea that we cannot change our mates, but we can change ourselves. Effect a positive change on yourself and you and your marriage will both benefit from it.

So — did you pack your own emotional bags?

By Heather V. Long
— Managing Editor, Families.com

L.O.V.E.

Leave in your wake what is pain centered in all human nature, in order to join another soul in a shared journey called life. Permit for yourself freely your God given right to love and to be loved.

— Charles Rivers

BOOK 1

Unclaimed Baggage

What Makes Good Love Hurt So Bad?

Most romantically charged relationships once red hot with passion become less than tepid warm without growth and even detrimental to the emotional states of both husband and wife. When loving committed relationships hit rock bottom, you might think planning a method of escape is the only logical solution for the pain you are causing one another. But I am here to tell you divorce is not the answer. If you choose to walk out on your spouse, you won't be avoiding the problems of marriage. In fact, you will actually be compounding those problems and concerns by taking them with you throughout your life. Most people carry their personal difficulties and baggage into their

1

sacred marriages and depart with them alive and intact after the divorce.

As adults, each and everyone one of us lives either for or against our childhood and upbringing. So if we treasured our experiences of youth, we will likely seek to share them with our spouse and children within marriage. On the other hand, if our growth experiences were perceived to be far more painful then we believed they ought to have been, then without forgiveness we will seek to bury that awareness. But covering up pain does not make it go away; in fact it intensifies with age if not properly healed, addressed, and forgiven. These unhealed spiritual wounds are enough to cause most people to lose their spouses long before losing the pains that cause people to flee from their presence.

But what about good people like yourself who are tired of letting those experiences dominate your life and even ruin your happiness? What about the beautiful spirits like yourself who engage in positive self help books and growth counseling because you desire to heal what you know is best for you're authentic self? Is it possible to resurrect the shared love you once held close to your shared hearts?

Yes, it is possible and if you earnestly put into practice what you learn here, I promise it will become permanent in your relationship, and not just for a season. What most of us need out of a failing relationship is an honest do over, a second time to make right what we failed at the first time .

Now how do we engage this relationship rebirth, how do we start this do over of two hurting spirits? First and foremost, withdraw any thoughts of flights of fancy towards divorce. Heading for the front door is far more painful than heading for any kind of face-to-face reconciliation. It is the avoidance and dismissal of problems that triggers the divorce and not the acknowledgement towards a sense of resolution. What a couple has dodged up to the moment of disillusionment is what has brought them to that point.

Whether I travel or teach relationship seminars locally, I find that most couples, bring far more issues and concerns with them to the marriage than they could ever, and I do mean ever, generate within it. In fact, I can honestly say I have never held a seminar or taught a marriage session where the problems were solely based in the relationship. Most problems, angers, and concerns were triggered by hurts and dislikes from their childhood past resurrectively reflected within their current marital life. Their fantasies of divorce were compelled by the need to escape the same troubles that had dominated their youth for many years.

> *Most complaints and*
> *concerns we have about our*
> *mates are really not as much*
> *about them as they*
> *are about us.*
>
> *— Charles Rivers*

The roots of anger, pressure, or stress originate from people's environments or circumstances are acting against their personal will, not Gods. Calmness can only be attained once people surrender their will for other people and their environment over to God from which they came. I know this as a husband, and if I find myself angered by or dislike something my wife does, I should easily be able to trace it back to not liking that same behavior in someone or something in my pre-married life. Unless I understand my path and use forgiveness

3

for those things upon that road I disliked, I can become hostage to trying to heal my past through assimilating my wife to what I feel makes me comfortable.

Unfortunately for us, unlike our real luggage our mental baggage can't be lost by the airlines. Through classes and seminars presented over the last decade, I have had the privilege of helping numerous couples effectively heal pain that would have once driven most people along a one-way road to divorce court. What follows are several true stories depicting the events surrounding the lives of couples who were negatively affected by past, unforgiving events. It is impossible to have a great marriage without letting go of the past through forgiveness but in holding fast to these negative memories, each person was, in fact, brought to the brink of losing their spouse.

Alex's Reality — Alex, constantly enjoys shouting down every good suggestion his wife makes as silly or without merit. He mocks her achievements as nothing more than the vanity of a spoiled little privileged kid. Shelly says she has no earthly idea where all of Alex's animosity and criticisms come from. Alex, when questioned about his criticism of Shelly, refuses to admit his comments are anything more than the innocent teasing all men do to their wives. All of Shelly's life, she has gone after her dreams with the support and backing of her parents. But lately she has begun to doubt her future dreams and the hopes of this marriage lasting past the present year. Every since she married Alex, she has found herself scaling back her goals so she does not overshadow his wishes for her.

Alex's Stowed Baggage — As a boy, Alex grew up in a home where his family routinely diverted him away from his natural talents in favor of him following in his father's chosen footsteps. When success didn't come for Alex in the field his parents selected for him, they deemed their boy a failure. As an adult, he recalled to me in one private session how he came to be attracted to Shelly. He commented she exhibited all of the high drive and determination he once possessed. Alex said to me, "*Shelly was one girl that used to stand up for herself no matter what people thought of her. But lately it seems that she has withdrawn from that passionate drive she once had. I'm doing everything I know possible to motivate her.*"

Alex did not realize he was the root cause for the change in Shelly's behavior. It was nothing he had set out intentionally to do at the beginning of the relationship, but it materialized over time because Alex had never addressed it prior to marriage. Unfortunately, Alex had not yet forgiven his parents for a wrong he perceived they visited upon him. Now his relationship is in ruins because he responds to his wife as his parents once responded to him. His envy of Shelly's achievements doesn't have much to do with Shelly—it has to do with Shelly's parents. What appeared to be envy of her achievements grew out of a desire for the more supportive upbringing Shelly experienced .

"A hurting
heart yields strife
in the presence of the love
it requires most."

— Charles Rivers

Nina's Reality — Nina was emphatic when she married her husband Pete that she would not tolerate adultery. Although Pete has carried a strict monogamous stance for marriage since he was a little boy, Nina's fears were not allayed. Nina, wanting to play it safe all her life, has been careful to marry a man who believes in strict monogamy — yet in still she has no trust in her husband's faithfulness. Over the last five years of marriage she has kept fears of betrayal close to her heart in hopes of staying sharp enough to catch her husband in the act. This type of behavior on Nina's behalf has destroyed every moment of closeness a loving relationship has to offer. Nina is prompt to tell Pete she does not trust his fidelity to her any further than knowing his whereabouts. Though she considers herself as a godly person, she refers to all men, including Pete, as dogs and unfaithful cheaters.

Nina's Misplaced Baggage — As a child, Nina was raised in a home where her father flagrantly cheated on her mother. Since the age of eighteen, Nina has had at least seven failed relationships prior to marriage with men she knew were habitually unfaithful. Her fears of a committed relationship grew in part out of what she witnessed between her parents marriage and have nothing to do with Pete. If Nina is unable to forgive her upbringing, she will continue to make her husband Pete pay penitence for the entire species of man.

Margaret's Reality — Over the last forty years, Margaret has grown to believe she is equal only to what she can attain by wealth or status. Not a weekend has passed where she has not made extremely high purchases on her credit cards in order to line the walls of her already overcrowded home. Margaret has been known to spend so many weekends at high-end stores that the employees at some have come to associate her as a family member. With a now overly hectic work schedule to support her booming lifestyle, she finds less and less time to spend with her now estranged family. Her conversations with her coworkers are little more than bolstering of what she owns or will attain next. Over the last ten years, Margaret's household has grown rich in material goods but impoverished in love because of the lack of intimacy money can't buy.

> *"For whatever is*
> *pressed down upon us*
> *becomes us, unless we are*
> *willing to forgive our*
> *trangressors."*
>
> *— Charles Rivers*

Margaret's Carry on Baggage — Margaret grew up in a time where the national economy took such a bad hit it caused both of her parents to become unemployed. To save money for critical needs, her parents imposed severe frugality over their spending habits. They withdrew Margaret from a private school and friends she had come to love. They sold a home that had been paid off and moved to a lower income neighborhood to devote their income to a mountain of debt acquired before the downturn of the economy. Margaret remembers going to school for many years in clothes from stores that sold only seconds. In Margaret's young mind, her parents were failures because they lost everything in her eyes. The fact that her mother had another child while their finances were low only cemented this in Margaret's mind.

She recalls that her parents did all they could to keep the family together back then, even though the finances were not. Margaret believed that she and her newborn sister dragged down the finances of the family. She thought that it would have been easy if her parents were free to pursue wealth instead of supporting children. Her parents did not recall this at all; what they remembered is that this was the best time in their lives. They recanted how this brought them back to understanding what was really important, namely family. Margaret did not receive that message, even though her parents had recovered far more than they lost only twelve years after the downturn.

Craig's Reality — Craig has entered his second year of marriage terse and bitter towards his wife, Monica. He identifies every serious discussion between Monica and himself as a personal attack on his manhood. Each attempt Monica makes to find resolution in the growing rift between them is met with the silence or indifference. Monica recounts that she has heard Craig say on many occasions that she will "never be able to dominate him as a man, so don't even try."

Craig's Unchecked Baggage — As a boy, Craig watched his mother browbeat his father on a daily basis throughout their marriage. None of Craig's extended family members knew back then why it was that Craig's father stayed with his wife. Viewing his parents locked in a loveless relationship, Craig promised himself that his marriage would never be that way. As an adult, his choice for a wife was completely the opposite of his mother's personality and demeanor. He remembers choosing to marry Monica over all of the other women he dated because she had a loving and gentle spirit.

But lately Craig has not been honoring that spirit. His deliberate rudeness to his wife extends from his erroneous belief that he will end up being bullied by his wife as his father was by his mother. Craig is now living the exact life that he had planned to avoid many years ago. The only difference is he is acting out the role of his mother instead of the position his father took. In fact, Craig unconsciously chose Monica because she would emulate his father's tolerance of awful behaviors.

Lisa's Reality — Lisa's marriage to her husband, Paul, has been teetering off and on the brink of separation for the last six months of a two-year marriage. In the beginning months of their new marriage romance between them had been wonderfully charming. But now that they have been married for only a short time, Lisa has begun to recoil from Paul's physical touch. Lisa explained to me that she does not mean to hurt Paul's feelings but that she does not desire this type of closeness with him or anyone else right now. Lately even Paul's gazes of admiration are becoming little more than painful stings of lust in Lisa's eye.

Lisa's Damaged Baggage — In what should have been the safest place on earth, Lisa was molested by her father in their home. Her perception of sex since has been tainted as nothing more than the filthy way men receive gratification. Sometimes the unforgiving pains of childhood hurt as many as five generations that follow the initial trauma. Childhood pains can affect your spouse just as much as they do you, for in marriage not only do you share names but pains, pleasures and past experiences.

To add insult to injury, as a little girl, Lisa had no comforting arms to fall into. She recounts with animosity how her own mother chose not to believe what was going on in the home. Determined to be free from her pain, Lisa chose Paul because he appeared to be a non-threatening caring man that could help her through her intimacy issues. But Paul can never succeed at helping Lisa as long as she keeps her history a secret from him.

Lisa, like many other people, became acutely aware of the pains she hides if they are reflected in life by everyday people like Paul. In her case, the advances of her husband mirrored the molesting advances of her parent. In fact, reflecting back becomes very dangerous because we end up focusing only on the hurt in the midst of great pleasure all around us. This sense of unresolved pain blinds our vision where our pre-hurt memories once gave us sight. This is why I adamantly tell all couples I get the chance to influence to turn your hurts and pains over to God. Because only God and the power of forgiveness allows us to lift the thin veil of blindness that has been blocking our sight to joy.

In John 9:25 we witness as the once blind man stands before the Pharisees virtually on trial for being cured on the Sabbath. He is questioned on the ethics of whether Jesus was a sinner due to the fact that he cured him on this holiest of days. His response to their accusations of blasphemy was simple when he said, "*I do not know whether this man is a sinner or what you say of him, but one thing I do know, I was blind but now I see!*"

I believe this healing was symbolic of what Jesus can do for all persons who have gone through pains or tragedy and have become blinded to what is the best in them and their relationships to the people closest to them. For this man had not done any sin that would call down the punishment of blindness. But in his healing of blindness he experiences the same release from bondage that anyone of us would from past injuries.

The Journey To Wellness Begins

In this the first book entitled *Unclaimed Baggage*, we are going to learn how to leave what was pain and self focused in our spiritual nature behind in order to grow with the one we have pledged our love vows to. All growth in life starts with a process of surrendering what we believed to be our harmful personal truths, not loves truth. So if your marriage has become stagnant you will have to leave the level of love you have become accustomed to in order to experience the next highest level of personal peace.

"For one does not mature primarily based upon who they are, but who they are not thus far."

— Charles Rivers

When Loss Is Gain

From the time of Adam and Eve to our present time, God has always required a person, a couple or a people to leave either who they are or where they are in order to make them great. The path to growth has always been one that is preceded by leaving of your old self behind. In the eyes of God, your marriage is no different. Anyone that God called to leave but failed to meet his expectations was either because they carried the mental baggage of where they came from or the stains of who they were injured by in their past with them.

Examine for yourself the biblical passages of those who were commanded to leave the old self behind to begin anew. When God calls upon us to leave, it will be for one of those same three reasons. It might be for our *health*, as when he sent the angels in Genesis 12:1-3 to tell Abraham to *leave Sodom* safely before he destroyed the town.

It might be for our *personal growth*, as when God told all men in Genesis 2:24 to *leave their fathers and mothers behind* and cleave to their wives. But the one command to leave that most people prefer to the others is the last: when the Lord tells us to leave for the sake of *gaining wealth*, as when he told Moses in Exodus 3:8 to leave Egypt and go to possess a land flowing with milk and honey that he will give the Israelites. Now if God the Father tells you to leave for all three reasons you may count yourself as blessed. But if he allows you to marry someone before leaving the person you are behind for spiritual growth you should count yourself as doubly blessed. For in doing this He is sending someone on the journey with you to comfort and keep you in times of plenty and in times of want for a greater purpose beyond your insight.

Controlling Behaviors Always Precede Conflict

On an absolutely beautiful autumn afternoon I was scheduled to receive a religious couple who were on the brink of divorce and had little faith left in the institution of marriage. I knew they were religious as I had lengthy conversations with both husband and wife on the phone prior to the face-to-face meet. The one request I remembered of both was that I would have to have to believe in God and be able to help them in a religious path to healing the strife in their marriage. I assured them that there would be no problem in this request although when I started out initially to help couples with my writings I would have believed it would be mainly secular. So I agreed to meet them and was most curious as to why their own place of worship could not help them. My wife and constant companion, Bridget, met this young couple at the offices of the building that housed my seminar classes. Bridget, as usual, saw to it that they were received as graciously as possible. Within a short time I joined them in the conference room, where we had developed a warm, loving aroma filled environment with catered meals for centering the attitudes of stressed out couples. This day would not be business as usual, for this couple would become my greatest inadvertent teachers of strife resolution in the institution called marriage.

I can't say that I remember ever being without words by the way I enjoy running my mouth when I teach. But I sat without words mesmerized in that conference room at the sight of two devout religious people cynically tearing each other apart with every fiber of their being. Husband and wife had a pad and pen with which they would jot down retaliatory strikes to be levied against one another's accusations. This was so that they could address each issue defensively and with strength while the other person ceased to speak for just a moment. I noted in my areas of Improvement log how, with the mastery of a tenured scholar, they easily quoted biblical verses in support of their past offenses in opposition to one another. On this day God and the bible would sit in defense of their misdeeds more than this couple would be willing to.

Not only could husband and wife successfully quote the passages and paragraphs of their bible but probably the line item with page number. For anybody this would be a difficult feat at best, but not for the Smiths, for they were raised in church. In fact, Tim's father was a minister his entire adult life until the day he died a few years earlier. What each spouse failed to understand was that they were doing little more than twist quoting the bible. For in no way does the bible justify bad behavior or strife between husband and wife as right living.

One verse in particular that Mr. Smith continually chose to twist quote in his favor was the same verse most religious men lean upon when they are being denied sexual relations by their wives.

Mr. Smith quoted to his wife, in my presence, the bible verse that states, *"For the wife's body is not her own but the husband's"* 1 Corinthians 7:4. In this belief, regardless of how tattered their relationship was, everything would magically heal itself if she would just go to bed with him. Sure they would despise one another, but his sexual desires would be fulfilled along with his need for what he perceived as love. Their relationship had run its course for eleven years this way and would not make it one more day under these conditions.

I knew for a fact that Mrs. Smith had her own personal issues (she was molested by her father as a child), but at least she was in pursuit of true love. But the true love she sought was from her father through other men as fatherly figures, which had resulted only in sexual love. By the time we met, Mrs. Smith confessed to me that she was tired of men altogether. She thought maybe if she could just settle for the divorce everything would be fine over time. She had held out hope for too long that her husband would show her true love. With each passing day, the more her husband refused to show real love the angrier she grew. There were several times in their private home when she would get so angry with herself that she would physically lash out at Mr. Smith. But in actuality, she was really lashing out at her father through her husband.

The Smiths were a couple seriously out of Gods will for

their love and therefore blinded to its power to heal their marriage. Mr. Smith had seriously misjudged the Creators intention for wife as nothing more than sexual property given to him by God to do with as he pleased. This alienated Mr. Smith from his own humanity by his misinterpretation of women in a spiritually companionate relationship. In coming to know Mr. Smith over some period of time, I would arrive to understand that his disrespect for his wife grew from his disillusionment with his own mother's behavior towards his late father.

Mr. Smith was silently angry with his mother for her resistance to his father when he was a minister. For all of the work his father did in the church, he could never sway Influence upon his resistant wife. In Mr. Smith's opinion his mother, "had always tried to steam roll her family contrary to every decision the father made." Even beyond Mr. Smith's father's death, the mother continued to interfere in the lives of her adult children. As an adult, Mr. Smith somehow reasoned it was his job to bully and convert his wife through domination of all forms because his father failed to effect change through positive means upon his spouse.

Mrs. Smith had her own inner turmoil to deal with that had lasted since her troubled youth. She still harbored hatred in her heart for her father, who had molested her as a little child. Her disdain for her husband was similar to many cases where the husband, in the mind of the wife, takes up where the father left off.

The Smith's difficulty was not that they couldn't achieve high marks at any religious academy for accuracy of religious doctrine. Their deficit was in they had no love for one another or themselves long before they ever came to pay me a visit. To have the ability to discern the biblical truth and

15

activate its power in your everyday life, you must have love. The Apostle Paul wrote to the church of Corinth that, *"If anyone imagines that he has come to know and understand much [of divine things, without love,] he does not perceive and recognize and understand as strongly and clearly, nor has he become as intimately acquainted with anything as he ought or as is necessary."* 1 Corinthians 8:2

Would Having More Sex or Attaining More Wealth Improve Your Relationship?

Nothing could be further from the truth. Even if every psychotherapist in the world took a vote and agreed upon it. Most adults have had sex numerous times prior to marriage. Within a marriage of some ten years or more, a couple may have had sex several thousand times. One more sexual moment would not add an ounce of love to a person's life. Therefore having sex with your spouse or anyone else could never make you sexually satisfied. The sense of satisfaction with who you are must come from a spiritual center within. One will never find permanent satisfaction with the physical relationship, for sexual love or erotic love is more of a state of mind aroused by the senses more then it being true love. Concerning money, you could follow the wages of a middle class family from the time they marry until the time of retirement and you may learn something that most people never consider: together a married couple could collectively make several millions of dollars over their lifetime. Even though many people may not be financially wealthy down the road, earning one more dollar would not draw any more love to their relationship because money in and of itself will not buy you inward fulfillment.

Traditional non-spiritual counseling fails couples because it originates from the reasoning's of man's mind minus the will of God. Traditional counseling seeks to implant theories and solutions into the consciousness of the human psyche. God's

Why Traditional Counseling Creates More Problems than It Solves

word, on the other hand, is infallible and in its purpose seeks only to pull clarification out of man's soul in order to activate his consciousness to love. Only God knows the heart of man, which is why he implanted solutions to the troubles that plague us in advance of our earthly birth on an individual case-by-case basis.

The non-spiritual counselor who does not acknowledge a higher form of love is the self appointed final approving authority on the message he/she seeks to impart upon you. If he/she does not draw their influence from God to heal your relationships, where do they get it? If it comes from self or psychoanalysis alone, then you are looking at the highest approving authority in your life. The bible tells us that, *"The plans of the mind and orderly thinking belong to man, but from the lord comes the [wise] answer of the tongue. All the ways of a man are pure in his own eyes but the lord weighs the spirit."* Proverbs 6:1

"What weight can any counsel
apply to the Instruction to forgive
if it does not originate from
the mouth of God?"

— *Charles Rivers*

But for true marriages the most priceless gift the Creator can bestow upon us is the gift of discernment. The spirit of relationship love discernment should be the most prized in any relationship over non-spiritual advice. For without this gift all else between the Creator and the created become lost in translation. The bible in the hands of the non-discernable of loves gifts becomes little more than a Shakespearean novel to be read cover to cover. In fact, we are cautioned about trying to understand the spirit of God through the natural man verses the spiritual man.

In 1ˢᵗ Corinthians 2:14 Paul tells us, *"But the natural, nonspiritual man does not accept or welcome or admit into his heart the gifts and teachings and revelations of the Spirit of God, for they are folly to him; and he is incapable of knowing them because they are spiritually discerned and estimated and appreciated."*

The Myth of Relationship Compatibility

Many recent studies have been done in the scientific communities that suggest that compatibility is best for marriage longevity. In fact this was one of the most common factors brought up by couples who came to see me as to why they were not getting along with one another. But after hearing both side of the conversation you could tell that most folk could not live well with anybody until they took the time to get their own ducks in a row. Compatibility is the new buzzword for I value my opinion only and all those who value my opinion only. But for sure it will not prevent you from arguing because most people's arguments are with themselves and not others. Compatibility, in my opinion has been the worst hoax ever perpetrated upon the institution of marriage since its inception. For if compatibility was the panacea of all marriage ills, as it is claimed to be, then why is the institution of marriage over six thousand years old? The very nature of the creation of man and woman dispels this belief. Because out of all of the Gods natural wonders, the human was the only being designed with a critically disagreeable intellect. Therefore it would take a huge stretch of the imagination for two freethinking persons to always agree on every decision.

When God felt Adams alone in the Garden of Eden he decided that he would fashion for him a suitable helpmate. Now here is where things get tricky for the scientific community concerning compatibility. God had a choice to create a clone-like being as Adam for a friend, cementing the premise of self-love, but he did not. Instead he created Eve, who was not only the complete opposite of Adam In body makeup and chemistry, but so were her thoughts, wishes and opinions. To make Eve completely compatible with Adam, you would have to either destroy her free will or make her brain respond only as an extension of Adam's thoughts.

This was not to be so in God's sovereignty, for even in the children that are born to marriage; each is born representative of their own hopes, dreams and aspirations. In all of God's creations, natural love combined with free will becomes the glue that holds the relationship together. God left intact the human marriage with the same frailties of free will that allowed the apple to be drawn from the tree of good and evil. He left it up to husband and wife to join and come to a consensus despite their backgrounds or incomes or head baggage.

This is important information for couples to know who wish no evil to ever befall their relationship. God took the same risk in the Garden of Eden that all husbands or wives do in placing their trust in the person they choose to love. That risk being that your greatest love may be pulled away from you by their unfettered free will despite our best quest for compatibility or harmony. If God believed in compatibility he would have made our human brains extensions of his control, thereby killing the concept of free will.

In 1st Corinthians 13:5 The Apostle Paul further dispels this myth when he writes, *"Love (God's love in us) does not insist on its own rights or its own way, for it is not self seeking."*

Further proof of the Creator's incompatibility theory is that no one has ever been born with the exact facial features or fingerprints of another. You could even have two twins grow up in the same home their entire lives and end up just as they started, completely incompatible. The scientific community has natural love wrong if they persist in reducing it to methodical formulas. In most cases, we place more consideration and planning into finding an employee for a new job position than in choosing a spouse.

Why? Because the employer seeks an employee who is compatible with his wishes and goals of the business motto. The employer wants an employee who will take orders at any time, day or night, without complaint. This type of working relationship for money is the opposite of free will and marriage. Compatibility is a flawed science for love, for it chooses love from the thoughts of the mind, while true love, chooses to love from the spirits center, the heart, which is blind to all formulas and sciences of the mind.

Marriage, is
not about control. In
fact, it is the opposite of control.
It exists on the realm of mysteries and
like a mystery only best when carefully
unfolded. Where as a controlled
environment becomes insistent
upon a very narrow
fixed outcome."

— Bridget Rivers

"One's unchallenged
comfort zone becomes little
more than an imprisoning wall to
the soul's ability to express
love freely."

— Charles Rivers

Most couples that seek separation do so with the idea that it will assist in the dissipation of a mountain of worry debt or hurt. When I receive couples who approach me with the belief that their problems are mountainous, I congratulate them. I congratulate them be-

You are Strengthened by the Problems You Resolve — and Weakened by those You Run From

cause a problem-free relationship is not really a relationship at all. Now they have something in common that is real to them. Pooling our faith in God during times of trouble or disagreements allows couples an assurance of a brighter tomorrow. We are promised by Jesus in Matthew 17:20 that, *"If you have the faith like a grain of mustard seed, you can say to this mountain, Move from here to yonder place, and it will move; and nothing will be impossible to you."*

So it is within the marriage relationship that couples can merge their faith and move any mountain together. Because in life problems will befall all relationships to draw the couple closer together — not pull them apart. Couples who believe

23

in a fantasy relationship get disappointed with each real life scenario that happens upon their home, even though they are powerless to avoid it. Each problem given by the universe presents itself upon our homes on an inclining scale.

These problems start low at one end and continue to climb with increasing intensity and sophistications until the couple jointly brings them to resolution. If a spiritual couple chooses not to answer its call to resolution, it will not go away. Couples who come to me with many problems that span several years usually believe things will never be resolved. But I have found in working with couples for the last decade that the opposite holds true. Some of the most painful relationships turn out to be more loving and binding after resolution then they ever were before.

A healed relationship is far more interpersonal then the original one we tried to live flawlessly under. Most relationships that part before the healing process divide under angered circumstances that taint society's view of the institution of marriage. In subsequent relationships each divorcee eventually end up putting their new spouse in the same old light as their spouses were made to be judged by. An angered divorced person will run them through many grueling tests at arms length to make them prove their love before reciprocating in kind. This type of behavior will only serve to invite the same pain they had sought to leave behind in the previous relationship.

24

*"When we allow past injuries
and pains to guide our daily existence,
we end up going forward in life
with a rear thinking mind set."*

— *Charles Rivers*

Before people can free themselves of the past pains that affect their current relationship they must first understand the power that fear has to damage love. Some mar-

Where There is Fear Present, Love Cannot Coexist.

riage relationships have a fear of past relationship failures. For example, your parent's relationship might have ended in divorce and divided an otherwise beautiful family. We become preoccupied with wondering whether these distressing experiences will affect our marriage now. Other couples have a fear of their present happiness fading away over time. This is frequently representative by a "we are so happy as a couple now; will it last?" syndrome.

Finally, most marriage relationships that fail become possessed by the remaining fears of the future. The fear of the future predicts that we will not be able to make it until parting by one spouse due to old age before we separate or divorce. This is because the current trend of relationship disillusionment convinces people that only past generations had that type of staying power. It leaves couples to wonder if they will destroy their children's lives by becoming divorce statistics. These fears destroy marriages at all stages because the home is being dom-

25

inated by an overemphasis of the emotion fear. If past fears in life threaten you or your home, you must excise them in order to save your relationship and your very life. Why? The Apostle Paul writes to Timothy, *"For God did not give us a spirit of fear, but of power and of love and of calm and well balanced mind and discipline and self control"* (2 Timothy 1:7).

Where there is fear present, love cannot coexist. Light and darkness cannot cohabitate the same space at the same time. Love comes from God, and fear from the devil. But whatever is greatest in your home will be the demise of the weaker. In 1st John 4:18 we are told, *"There is no fear in love (dread does not exist), but full-grown (complete, perfect) love turns fear out of doors and expels every trace of terror! For fear brings with it the thoughts of punishment and (so) he who is afraid has not reached the full maturity of love [Is not yet grown into loves complete perfection].*

"One can never
Truly experience the
Abundant fruits of love whose
heart remains guarded by
past hurts and fears

— Charles Rivers

The Path to Energizing Anemic Love

The best example I can give you to infuse spiritual love in a hurry into your relationship has existed since the dawn of man. We will model this behavior throughout this book and your life to heal your closeness as a spiritual couple. We will be discussing this knowledge key more in depth in Chapter 2, entitled *Domestic Baggage*.

But I must say that no matter whether I am giving a one on one marriage enrichment session with a husband and wife, mass seminars or radio addresses, I always ask this question first:

*"Why is it that a typical friendship
is capable of lasting twenty years,
while a marriage is hard pressed
to last barely two?"*

— Charles Rivers

Now I have received varied answers to this question over the many years I have taught this course in love. But for some reason the answers usually come back to me in the form of rhetorical questions. They are what I jokingly refer to as questionable answers. I receive answers such as, "Isn't it because friends don't live together and that is why their relationship last longer then marriages?"

But the true answer to that question is the solution to all of your relationship problems as well as true loves solution for the unhealed relationship. I further suggest to husbands and wives that my instruction be used to change themselves and not their spouse. Just as easily as you picked up this book and made it a tool for change in your life, so can your spouse.

*"All true change
occurs from within and
not from without."*

— Charles Rivers

Let's observe what happens when you try to force change upon a person concerning something that they are dead set against. Let me use an example most of us are familiar with namely "eating what we thought was bad food when we were children." How many of us remember sitting for long periods at mom's kitchen table because we refused to eat our vegetables? At a young age children will take a liking more to sugars than they ever will to vegetables or what is right for them. As parents, we end up looking like the bad guy as we try to induce our children to do or eat right.

But no amount of prodding or willpower will ever inspire our children to convert to doing something they don't want to do willingly. In fact, if you put pressure on your children beyond a certain limit, you risk hurting them or permanently setting them against ever liking what you are trying to promote that is healthy for them in their lives. The same applies to you forcing your spouse to give you love as you believe he or she should or changing one of their negative behaviors to a positive one.

If one spouse tries to force-feed his or her opinions or views of life on the other without the power of love, he or she risks solidifying inaction regarding that problem. It is easier to elicit a negative response from someone's behavior by force-feeding a behavior than it is to get positive. But to change someone from negative to positive requires your support and true spirit filled love. Anything less will be short-lived or something other than genuine behavior.

*"There is no challenge
in loving someone who
loves you back."*

— *Charles Rivers*

I was once asked for guidance by a man who was completely frustrated with his wife's soured attitude concerning him and their marriage. But he truly loved her and above all else he wanted to see her happy

Don't Give Up On The Relationship Just Yet

but he did not know how long he should wait for her to come around to the love he knew she really possessed inside. Neither one of them had cheated on one another or fought one another physically, so I knew immediately what my advice would be to him. I told him to give her another eighteen years before he entertained any thoughts of giving up on the relationship.

At that moment he looked at me like I was just the craziest thing on the planet. "Another eighteen years? Are you sure about that?" "Yes," I said, "give her another eighteen years at the minimum without any consideration of what may happen." Then I proceeded to explain to him what that number symbolized. You see, most people grew up in the home of their mother; others may have had to live with a grandparent or relative. But during those growing years you had a parent who cared for you when you were not at your best. When you were transitioning through your rebellious or angry stage.

"Which of the Saints had
The sweetness of the Spirit
without experiencing bitterness.
Therefore one who craves
sweetness must not flee
fom things that
are bitter."

— *Saint Birgitta of Sweden*

Those were the parents who stood by us when we did things that were detrimental to our safety and our future successes. They loved us when we were unlovable, because any parent worth their salt knows one thing: when it comes to children, there is no challenge in loving someone who loves you back. The challenge is in loving your child through them hating you until they come around to becoming what was best in them. So yes, I expected him to stay with his wife the same way his mother stayed with and loved him. I knew that this one man had the calmest demeanor to be able to carry that through easily where most other guys couldn't last much longer with this same person. Additionally I knew that she wasn't really a bad woman after all, but just a person trying to find herself by pealing off past layers of stinking hurt, all she needed was time. I am grateful to report that he is now living up to that eighteen-year period of reciprocal support. I similarly expected his wife to change her behaviors and show him true love in kind.

The relationship of the lover to the loved is never a tidy one as much as it is a fluid one. Stressful situations between couples at some point are just precursors to dealing with stressful situations that will be brought your way by your children at all stages of their growth. We are called by the Creator to grow up, out or through the trials that life brings our way and not to run from them or the people closest to us. The loves challenged need the love more so than the love filled. Jesus Christ speaks to the Pharisees and Scribes who were grumbling against the way they saw him casually eating and drinking with people they considered sinful, His reply was, *"It is not those who are healthy who need a physician, but those who are sick"* Luke 5:31. Meaning that he was not sent to save the saved but to save those who had been lost.

> *"Love has a*
> *very short shelf life;*
> *ensure that you give it away*
> *before it goes bad."*
>
> — *Charles Rivers*

Our Problems Are Not My Fault!

Many husbands and wives attending my relationship sessions sincerely came with an honest belief that they were guiltless of all the problems in a shared relationship. I let couples who came to my office know that I do not believe in the blame game and I would not allow them to play it with each other either. Blame will only hold you hostage to unresolved issues. One thing is for sure: once poison, hatred or bitterness has crossed our collective doorstep, it will remain the full time job of both partners to individually and cooperatively eradicate it.

Even if we believe ourselves to be the guiltless one, trust me when I say the experience has changed you. As a husband and father, I can catch and bring home the flu (a metaphor for bitterness and cynicism) and, without knowing, easily spread it to my wife and children. But to get the house cured of this illness will require a collective effort on the parts of all of its inhabitants: including the children.

Sure, I could go out and purchase the flu medicine needed to heal myself (spiritual counseling/self help books), but I could never heal my family with all of the medicine I take. I would have to make that love I learned about genuine by putting it into actions. To heal my home, I could bring soup (a metaphor for love), juice and cool towels to my wife and children until my family was back to wellness. Once we have regained strength as a family, we could disinfect the entire house by letting true love into our home to guard against future viruses.

*"Hatred is like taking a
poisonous pill and expecting
the other person that you aim
that hatred at to die."*

— Author unknown

"Love endures long and is patient and kind; Love never is envious nor boils over with jealousy, is not boastful or vainglorious, does not display itself haughtily."

1 Corinthians 13:4

In all relationships that are unhealed, couples argue and disagree depending on where their belief of true love relationships lies within them. For some people the relationship lies within the heart and for many others it exists merely in their heads. If you can locate where your opinion of love resides within your person, you will

You Will Remove a Mountain of Dirt In A Bad Relationship Before You Reach Gold

have resolved half of your love problems. Is your relationship in your head or in your heart? A relationship that rests in your heart is a loving one. A relationship that resides in the head is of a controlling nature or a reasoning of the mind over the spirit.

A relationship in the heart (your spiritual center) says: I brought you these flowers as a symbol of the love I feel for you. A relationship in the head says: I brought you these flowers because I am trying to manipulate you for something I have done or need done down the road. A relationship in the head rations out its love over timed mandatory calendar events throughout the year. If you are in a relationship that

33

is not based in the heart, do not dismay for everyone is born with a redemptive nature that leads us back to the heart.

If you or your spouse has turned negative, a more positive nature is just a pick and a shovel away. If we are to get to the real worth or gold of any relationship, often times we will have to remove a lot of dirt, rocks and silt. If left alone, these problems creep up to choke the life's blood out of all loving relationships. If left unaddressed, we penalize our spouses in place of the actual people who caused us these harms initially.

The Properties of Gold are the Same as the Attributes of Love

God's love, as inherited by man, is eternal and always has a redemptive nature. Did you know that gold is the only substance that does not oxidize or corrode? In fact, most space missions that launch satellites have wires that use gold as a conductor and as a heat shield, instead of any other element. Scientists know that the rigors of constant heat and cold wreak havoc and corrode all other alloys but gold.

This is also why the gold on the satellite, in some cases, is worth more than its technology. This is chiefly because the components of the computers will fail long before the gold turns a half century old unblemished. That is why its alloy is the best representative of love. In 1st Corinthians 13:4 it states that, "love never fails or becomes obsolete or comes to an end." This is the strength of gold as well. Why then would we settle for less in our marriage relationships than we do with our personal wealth?

Many good people by the time they reach the legal age to marry enter relationships by going through the same processes as a person looking for effortless gold. Most of us are content to settle for pyrite or what is known as fool's gold. Fool's gold or (Iron Sulfide) mimics the consistency

End Your Search for False Gold

of true gold with the exception of three properties. The first is that it is found mostly on the surface of the ground, fooling those who discover it. The promise of finding effortless gold is the same as the premise for finding effortless relationships. Secondly, it tarnishes over a short time in the oxygen rich atmosphere — unlike true gold that would not over a million years. Lastly, while it is initially appealing to the eye, it is as brittle to the touch as it is merely made up of minerals that coat the outside surface of the gravel.

Pyrite is sadly representative of many shallow relationships that refuse to go beyond the surface. To do so would only serve to disturb the relational dirt that rests just beneath the physically attractive level of all beginning relationships. But if you desire a true and lasting relationship, you are going to have to be content with digging deep — for that is where the twenty-four karat gold called true love resides. God the Father placed gold, diamonds, silver and some of the most precious minerals and oil deep within the earth's protective mantle. God also placed your greatest wealth — your heart and spirit — deep within your chest cavity. That is why the Creator judges us by the heart and not the surface. So to activate the love in you or anyone else you must be willing to get dirty. For no human will yield their true self to you unless you are willing to understand what is most secret to them without giving the second judgment of their character, of the first being their own.

*"He who values
merely surface beauty
over true love heaps his wealth
upon an ever depreciating asset."*

— Charles Rivers

The human species, on the other hand, is more impressed with surface beauty but is dismayed once that beauty fades like the surface of pyrite (fools gold). Others run once they find out that dirt is under that shallow pyrite relationship. But mankind is not consistent in its nature of surface love. For man who does not honor true love will run out on a relationship that presents trouble for him beyond a set limit of time. It becomes not worth the effort, sweat and toil to see it through to the gold portion of the relationship that only comes with longevity. But if you take that same person and put him in charge of a gold mine, he will move a mountain of dirt for fifteen years, straight through some of the harshest and life threatening conditions for one bar of gold.

It's intriguing that men and women both are impressed when it takes fifteen years to dig one bar of gold out of the side of a mountain. But far impressive still is our God, who would stick that same bar of gold up to one half mile deep into that mountain's side. God has buried in you very precious treasures and gifts that may take years to uncover, depending on how much dirt you are willing to remove. But first each of us must be willing to venture deeper than surface appearances and emotionally guarded relationships.

There is a kindred knowledge to all living things that are under the essence of God's natural creation. If you learn what is common to the love of one, you can conquer the love of all. Nothing under the natural created hand of the Father's love will reveal itself to you unless you passion-

How Do I get My Spouse to Yield Their True Worth to Me?

ately love it first. The reason for this is because God made those living breathing people, pets or plants passionately in love and in passionate love only can they be activated to yield love to you. Consequentially those same living breathing entities are designed to resist you vigorously if you show them hate. The bible explains to us in Genesis 1:31 the feeling of contentment God had for what he created in the earth, *"And God saw everything that He had made, and behold, it was very good and He approved it completely."* So if you are in the company of one of God's creations and you disapprove of it, then it will not yield to you its abundance (its gold).

Have you ever tried to grow a plant without love and have it prosper? At the same time, you could live next door to a neighbor who loves plants and has the ability to grow eight foot hedges from a dying mass that stretches into your property line? Have you ever tried to keep a tank of gold fish only to have them die on you a school at a time — time and again — while a friend of yours is successful at not only getting their fish to live for years on end but also breeding them with little or no effort? Have you ever been in a relationship with someone that is unfruitful for you, yet the next person in that person's life is able to have them bear much fruit? In fact you might witness that same person moving into a large-sized home, having two children, and becoming very successful.

These are the people who are very successful at knowing how to release the gold in all they come in contact with. These are lovers who could bring a starving dog from the brink of starvation to a prestigious pedigree winner. They could nurse an ailing shrub from a stick to lush leaves with full aromatic blooms. More importantly, they could adopt an abused child, who has a very derogatory attitude, and turn she or he around to being the most positive and fruitful person on the face of the earth.

If God's creations do not bear fruit they are either not planted in the right location or they are estranged from love through rebellion. So all you need to learn right now is how to move your relationship to the right spiritual garden to grow, such as Adam and Eve possessed in the Garden of Eden. To do this, you will have to come to the realization that there is so much more to be changed within you than you could ever hope to achieve in changing your spouse.

Prepare yourself first to be healed if you will ever muster the will to command influence in mending your relationship. I want you to ask yourself the question that follows in italics from an honest loving heart rather than a protective posture. For if you read it this way I promise you will feel the hurt and pain of a lifetime lift immediately from your consciousness.

*"If my spouse was currently
my best friend in the world, could I
get away with treating them the
way I do now or would I
myself have to
change?"*

— *Charles Rivers*

What was your initial reaction to your brains answer to this question? Did you not feel immediately the many years of blame switch from your spouse's shoulders solely to a shared responsibility? Do not deny yourself this true feeling of the heart and mind. If you should ever falter resist change in repairing this relationship feel free to reread this question again. Now if you take this calling to heart then you can successfully compare the way you treat your best friends to the way you relate to your spouse. Countless persons all across the globe, like yourself, get people to do just about anything by being a true loving friend over being in opposition to them. Can you imagine that one child can get another to jump off a high ledge with a skateboard just because he is a best friend? Do you realize with a mere suggestion one friend can get another to go through college and complete a doctorate degree in a field that they feel unsure on? You too can have the power to grow that plant from death or activate the life in your spouse if you love them from the heart as two friends love one another.

Why Do Loving Couples Drift Apart?

Once loving couples decide to get married and merge homes together something bizarre takes place between them that has the potential of destroying the relationship. In their newlywed minds, they begin to wonder out aloud about future events. One is concerned about retirement, some forty plus years away. The other begins to vocalize how they need a larger home and better community standards for a child who has yet to be conceived. These ideas towards the future are beautiful and innocent enough, but not when they take on a life that will eventually overshadow the marriage relationship itself.

The very security a family sets out to attain can become the same goal that undermines the entire family. A newly-wed husband takes on as many additional hours at work for as much extra income as his job will allow an entire staff. He seeks to provide a higher standard of living for his family then the level he married at. What the husband does not cover financially, his wife can more than cover with overtime at her job. Now the couple who once had love for one another that was not based on finances begins to base their future love and happiness on money. They are proud to know that not only can they afford a new house but also everything they ever dreamed possible to go into that new home.

This behavior is what I refer to as building the *Tower of Babel* to heaven in your own home. Once intelligent people lean too heavily upon the concept of believing that wealth creates heaven, every item purchased becomes a brick contributing to the height of that tower. The residents of Babel did not want to wait to get to heaven. They were insistent upon having heaven and earth at the same time. They became no longer interested in the trip as much as the destination. This is the same fallacy of couples who become future — focused and present — dead.

Two years further down that same *Tower of Babel* road and the realities of how much money it will require turns that couple's dreams into a nightmare. Outrunning the interest on all of those new purchases brings depression and bickering for that once newlywed couple. The purchases they were making to enrich their own lives are doing little more than enriching the lives of the corporations they purchased them from. In fact, the more wealth they reach for without being conscious of the relationship the more impoverished their real love becomes. Now don't get me wrong — there is absolutely nothing wrong with acquiring wealth or nice things. I love beautiful cars, homes and just about anything you could buy as a creature comfort. But if we travel together on a journey called marriage and get lost along the way, we forget what the trip is truly about.

When that happens, we are no longer committed to one another in a relationship but to what we owe the creditors and most certainly to the whims of our employers, who have become the middlemen to finance our debts. Once the job becomes more important than the relationship, it will be easily said that Johnny and his wife Jane are two very dull people. It will take a major calamity or an illness at this point before a couple feels that they can sever their ties to a job to support one another, as they should.

Observe
from the senses
what your spouse's needs,
desires, pains and tribulation of the
heart really are. This will become a lifetime
journey that cannot be shortened for quick
answers any more than your own search for
meaning can be. In observing someone
outside of self you can grow to understand
self and the changes that must take
place within each of us.

Domestic Baggage

"The mind understands what the heart refuses to, while the heart deduces what the mind may never comprehend."

— Charles Rivers

In this book, entitled *Domestic Baggage*, I am going to make known to you how to improve your relationship with the God-given talents you already possess but have become estranged to.

The Secret to Living Happily Ever After

Before anyone can enjoy the trappings of relationship they must move from the outside looking in to dwelling among desirable companionship. In order to do that one must learn the basis for all permanent relationships, and that is that they start with a healthy fostering friendship. No relationship on the face of this earth reaches the age of understanding without friendship as its base. In Genesis, Adam and Eve are not long a couple in the Garden of Eden before friendship is commanded of man to woman. Genesis 2:24 states, "*It is not right that man should be alone, therefore a man shall leave his father and mother, unite to his bride and cleave to her and the two shall become one flesh.*"

The key to Adam's happiness or the modern day male is in deciphering this one authoritative verse. God is an awesome God indeed and he knew, long before all of the books that social scientists and I write concerning relationships, what to do to keep love alive within His own creation. For this reason, most marriages don't have to go beyond this verse to heal any rift a modern marriage has to offer — because normally after understanding this verse many people will come to know that they were only married by contract before understanding it.

The day you embrace it is the first day of marriage; regardless of if you have been married one or one hundred years. This is precisely the reason why most of what social science has done over the past half century towards marriage has failed. For their methods in their original intent were not created in love but mainly tactics in response to a hurting human condition. Science seeks to manage the pains that humans have, where true love seeks to liberate us from those confinements of a hurting spirit.

You see no relationship between men and women (that has thrived about six thousand years before modern day psychology) will be fixed by anything other than information directly from the Creator to the created. The Creator also knew that as men we would become pretty much bull headed in our relationships towards our wives without the gift of true spiritual love. It would be a difficult proposition at best for any man to keep a marriage together unless he applied this love applicable verse of friendship over stewardship to his relationship.

Let us understand the methodologies of the heavenly Father's chemistry of love. This is self evident by breaking down Genesis 2:24. It states, *"Therefore a man shall **unite** to his wife,* (the word *unite* involves the marriage ceremony only) *and cleave to her"* (the word cleave involves far more than just sticking close to her). In English, the definition of cleave means literally to remain faithful. A further clarification involves being steady in affection, loyal and a faithful friend.

Any Man Who Cleaves In Devotion Wins His Wife's Affections and Love for a Lifetime

So cleave, as directed by the founder of relational love, meant for Adam to be steady in allegiance and a close friend to his wife. Not the run of the mill average friendship that you see around you every day, but one that would stand head and shoulders above the strongest outside of the home relationship. The capstone of this verse is revealed when it is for told that after cleaving to her, *"the two shall become one flesh."* The couple over time would draw to become one as physical bodies, mind and spirit in line with their needs and limitations. The final stage of marriage would be in loving one another as God loves us, which cannot be achieved through the basic wedding ceremony or applying a ring to ones finger alone.

For even familiar love on its best day can change with the stresses of life. But it is when familiar love is buffeted by Gods love that any hurt feelings can be forgiven and people can be understood for who they are and not what they say and do in response to pain. So our heavenly father knew full well that just the wedding ceremony alone would not make two people a great couple. What would make an unbreakable bond is a friendship allegiance over time in line with pains, troubles and built in differences. That is the lynch pin of the verse when it is says that we become one flesh. The word become does not represent an immediate act, but a manifestation of events over time.

Still need Convincing on Friendship?

Let me magnify for the friendship disbeliever the only two titles mentioned in the bible concerning husband and wife. The first is the word *companion* spoken of many times in the old and new testaments. In Malachi 2:14 it states, *"She is your companion and wife of your (marriage) covenant."* You might notice how in the verse the two titles are distinct. It recognizes that the husband and wife are friends and married at the same time. The definition of the word companion is the same as the definition of the word friend. The other definition used in the bible is to represent a spouse is *helpmeet* or in the English language *helpmate*. The definition of the word helpmeet or helpmate is exactly the same as the word friend.

Sowing the Seeds of Love

Everyone is a lover of someone, somewhere at sometime in our world today. Don't be fooled for one minute by societal chants that love is dead. Love is not only alive but it's hidden within some of the most unexpected environments and just waiting for someone to tap into it and strike it rich. Most of us exercise on a daily basis a love for someone whether they know or appreciate it.

There is never a wrong time or mode of exercising genuine love unless that love remains only for self to the exclusion of all others. All of us possess the gift of love; however we are not guaranteed it will be returned in the capacity we desire to be loved in without effort. For if we were to be rewarded in such a manner then the light of love that uplifts us all from the depths becomes cheapened by the confines of our imagination to expect guaranteed love.

True love is greatest when it originates from the heart without the policing expectations of the ego or the head. For all love that births from the intellect over the heart becomes predestined to failure with the passing of each adoring thought. While the heart through its purest form of love fashions its anchor against the unavoidable storms that crash in opposition to each innocent coupling of the loved and the lover.

Love Births All Good Seed

Each time I teach a class on relationship happiness I am always inadvertently asked one question: "If friendship is so good for relationships then, why can't men and women start out as friends?" That observation would be simple enough if it were not for the fact that physical features, sex or a sense of closeness that reflects nothing of same sex friendships basically attracts men and women to one another. Most couples start out at the first love passionately but fewer and fewer graduate to the last in tact. I believe this to be due to the fact that over the last half-century people are moving away from true love towards a form of self love. But ultimately self love will abandon people, leaving them lonely in the heart and lonely in the end, while true unadulterated love allows people to be surrounded by a loving family and true friends now and through their last days. Many of us balk at giving up the Erotic (sexual) type of love for true love because we feel we have something to lose in our sexual life together. Actually, if we don't progress beyond the Initial sexual love phase, we will know only loss in our human relationships. For couples who cannot see their spouse as God's love sees them can only see them as tools to use or objects towards sexual gratification.

I challenge anybody who thinks that moving towards true closeness and harmony as loss to libido to try spiritual love in conjunction to erotic love. You will find out that no level of religiosity that the human species can achieve will ever kill your sex drive within a committed relationship. It was never meant to be that way in a committed relationship. I have been married to my wife for the last twenty years and she makes me even more sexually charged now then when I had no spiritual love for her or myself.

The Three Immutable Laws of Love

These three loves are defined from the Greek language as *Eros love*, (sexual love or desire). *Philia love*, (A friendship love arriving from close association), and *Agape love*, (Existing as the love God has for man and mankind for God and other humans). Once two people decide that they are interested in one another they experience feelings based primarily in Eros love or an erotic-type infatuation. Men and women alike have a tendency to focus on romantic love as all encompassing, but this is merely the start of love's bloom.

Eros or sexual love although pleasurable is a very poor substitute for real love. Although it provides a fine start for a young couple's blossoming relationship, it makes for a bad ending if they insist on making this love primary over the last two. Any relationship that is based purely on hormone driven erotic love will end with the waning of this love or once someone more attractive comes along. We must not see these three loves as separate and apart, but as a bridge to final relationship success.

The longest road all relationships must cross in order to find ultimate happiness passes over the bridge of Philia (friendship)

Bridging the Communications Gap

love. The two opposing anchors of that bridge of friendship we must cross are Eros (sexual) love and Agape (true) love. They hold up the bridge span of Philia (friendship) love. The reason your love should seek to endeavor higher than Eros love is because any relationship that is more passionate in the horizontal then vertical does not sustain spiritual growth but actually destroys it.

The support span of Philia or friendship love, as interpreted in English, becomes the healing point that all relationships that have languished too long in an erotic arena must cross. In this initial stage of relationship restitution you must exercise the same spirit of dynamic love, care and kindness that you extend to your other friends. Philia love should be used as a guide towards your final destiny, which is a relationship based upon Agape (true) love. Philia love, although more of a communicative love, should never be seen as a final destination in marriage.

The final destiny to strive for in your relationship is Agape love. Agape love is what older couples the age of our great grandparents needed to make it until they breathed their last. Agape love is the purest, non-sexual love in nature. It is the love that God extends towards man and man reciprocates towards God and his fellow human beings. This is the type of love that will forgive any misgivings, large or small, as surely as God forgives us. This love is equivalent to how we extend forgiveness to our out-of-the-home best friends when they wrong or slight us.

*"Most people
who have world class
relationships with friends
without Agape love struggle
at basic communication
with their spouse."*

— Charles Rivers

A Conniption
of Loves

In fact I would say that Agape (true) love is the only state of being that will let you love the person just because they exist even if they are displeased with you. I was once asked by an angry man how were we supposed to be friends with our spouses when we are married to them. He believed that marriage itself was a simple solution to covering all ills and communication conflicts from two strange persons that join together. That sounds good on paper but true love can never be sustained or influenced solely by placing a ring on your finger or a tattoo of the persons name on your body. Real love takes commitment and work just like real friendships. Most friendships require more love and trust and you couldn't sustain them treating the person like you do your spouse with or without a friendship ring.

God did not give us all three loves to parcel out as we deemed necessary. Never was the intention in marriage to love God in one way, your spouse in another, and your friends in a separate fashion. Marriage was designed to encompass all three loves working simultaneously in concert with one another. To design the way you love based upon your environment becomes a schizophrenic way of dividing up your consciousness. All three loves are needed in a combined fashion to make our marriages mature into a reflection of true love. If we offer only erotic love to our spouses, friendship love to the world, and Agape love to God, we become little more than character actors upon the stage of conditional love.

Couples that are facing constant strife and division at home must be prepared to move their relationship to higher ground. In

Bring Your Relationship Above the Belt if It is to Last

fact, each unresolved issue we face in marriage is in some shape, form or fashion a cry to move our love to a higher level. Judge for yourself all of the long-term relationships you have ever had

51

in your life where you experienced growth: your coach, your best teacher, your best friend. All of these relationships were non-sexual in nature. It was precisely because those relationships existed above the belt that you are who you are or where you are today. It is impossible to have true forgiveness for anyone that you have only sexual feelings for be that someone you are dating or someone you are married to.

It was the interpersonal relationships that made the longest lasting impressions upon our lives and spirit. All of the people we allowed into our lives to share a friendship relationship were able to impart wisdom, laughter or add balance to our life. Why? Because it is within the Philia (friendship) relationship that you and I can be motivated to change our thoughts and opinions about one another and consequentially about life.

Now contrast this with all of the dating and sexual relationships you experienced in your youth with the opposite gender. Did you learn half as much or anything long range from those types of Erotic relationships? Why not? Because you will never be able to successfully connect your feelings and open-mindedness to a purely physical relationship. In fact, you will remain at the whims and controls of your thoughts and body chemistry over a true higher calling to love.

Increase Your Sense of Deservedness

Sometimes in seminars I find the hardest thing to do is give some one the impetus to stay in an other than positive relationship long enough to resolve key issues. In other dating relationships it is usually hardest to motivate someone to leave someone who has little or no value for them. Let me show you how you can improve the one and drop the other if need be.

Look back in your youth at your first salaried job. This can be something as small as a paper route or a summer position in an office or a fast food restaurant. Based upon the age of the reader of this book will also date how small that first salary was. But let's just assign a number of $4.50 an hour for starters. Now throughout your growing years you slowly move up and get promoted or move on to a higher position. But ultimately everybody who desires a higher income will achieve the limits of their desires.

That is where your relationship comes in. For you see today your base salary may be far from that small potatoes of an income. Suffice to say if I asked you to take a job at $4.50 now knowing all you know I guarantee you would be insulted. Why? Because over time you have increased your sense of what you deserve from a job or career. Because of your current lifestyle your ego or way of living cannot afford to be paid pennies without getting evicted. So why would you settle for less in marriage? If you are currently experiencing a desire for improvement in your relationship go for it and make it happen just as you would a career.

You would not wait on the sidelines for someone else to act before you went for a promotion, then why would you sit back and wait for your spouse to improve before your relationship does. If you are dating and not married this news is especially important to you. Because if you are trying to grow a million dollar career with a person that has no value for you or themselves you are out of balance. You have increased your financial sense of deservedness but waxed over what you personally feel that you are worth.

Why Do People Drift to the Siren Song of Erotic Love?

Unfortunate for all of us who buy into this type of Erotic relationship don't realize that they are sure to fail if we insist on repackaging sexual love as true love. Advertising seeks to sell you Eros (sexual) love because it grabs the attention of the viewers' minds when a product cannot sell easily in an already overly crowded market on its own merits. Erotic (sexual) love works as a good selling tool in a rush, rush society because it is short term — and in most areas of love we have grown accustomed to short term. But Philia (friendship) and Agape (true) love are long term and you can not readily sell a quick society on long term love without introducing them to their own heart centered spirit first.

"In Agape, one can not be in love as much as one becomes love."

— Charles Rivers

Sex Enhances the Marriage But Divides the Dating Pair Bond

Most people have come to understand that sex ruins the friendship relationship between men and women. That may be so for single couples who date or live together, but it is the exact opposite for married couples. Never were the strengths of the three universal loves more important then when I had to give guidance to a minister's wife who had, over time, come to despise her husband for his attitudes of past.

She told me in no uncertain terms that she had moved out of their shared room to take up residence down the hall with her teenage daughter. She said she didn't mind being married to him just as long as they stayed in separate rooms and he didn't have to put his hands on her sexually. Teaching over many years on this one subject of relationships I have noticed that at least seventy percent of my audience claims for themselves a measure of religiosity. But also this was the widest audience that had the biggest problem with acting in a relationship what they knew to be right. This was a shock to me because initially I never started out over a decade ago to do anything more than to help non-spiritual couples because I was one myself and I thought we had the biggest problems. This proved to be reverse thinking and especially in the case of the ministers wife. Oddly enough, she felt she still loved God with all her heart. She carefully baked cookies and cooked for the church on a weekly basis. She would rush off to support any family in distress within the church with pride while allowing her marriage relationship to languish through neglect. After gathering a clearer picture of what she thought was her home condition I asked her about her understandings on the teachings of the three forms of love. She had only a vague recalling of a misinterpretation of all three but not a belief that they were anything else than something that was committed to paper. After clarifying to her the three forms of God-given love I showed her how it would be virtually impossible for her to hate her husband on the one hand and love God on the other. Because if she had achieved love for God, being the Agape (true) love level, she could not in good conscience turn

MARRIAGE WITHOUT BAGGAGE

to her husband and have none. For if people have truly reached an Agape (true) level of love, they have learned to respect all people despite their past behaviors. They have learned what it means to love people outside of their personal comfort zone. A person at an Agape (true) love level of consciousness understands what was meant in the biblical quote, *"For all have sinned, and come short of glory of God." Romans 3:23.* This verse alone indicates that God knew we were imperfect and so we should not judge each other in the context of perfection.

> *"No one can be all loving*
> *and yet all hating at the same time;*
> *that person will live in constant conflict*
> *inside of themselves more so than*
> *with the person they find*
> *hatred for."*
>
> *- Charles Rivers*

Moreover, if we hate anyone outside of ourselves, we hate God himself. Why? For in Genesis 1:26, God says, *"Let us [Father, Son, Holy Spirit] make mankind in our image.* In Genesis 1:27 we are given further clarification of this image of beauty. We are told, *"So God created man in his own image, in the image of God created he him; male and female created he them."* It is proof positive; I believe that if you look at anyone with anything less than Agape (true love), you hate not only him but his Creator as well. For one cannot hate the creation of a thing without hating its creator for inventing it.

So in being indifferent to her husband and loving anywhere else her conflict rested within herself and not by anything he could do. Not only did she find fault with her husband, but the structure of the marriage relationship. If only she was aware that she was sending God the message that she disbelieved in two of his creations, [her husband and marriage] but that she loved herself. God will not honor any relationship in this form of piousness double standard. Our heavenly Father would not be true to his word if he honored your dishonoring of the union of his creation.

In Galatians 6:6-8, it states, *"Do not be deceived and deluded and misled; God will not allow Himself to be sneered at (scorned, disdained, or mocked by mere pretensions or professions, or by His precepts being set aside.) [He inevitably deludes himself who attempts to delude God.] For whatever a man sows that and that only is what he will reap."*

God is love and since we are of God's creation we are love if we abide in the belief of true love. But if we live by the demonstrative examples set by Satan we become what Jesus criticized Abraham's descendents as being for not accepting his love, *"Children of the devil."* In addition, we are told further in 1 John 3:9-11, *"This is how we know who the children of God are and who the children of the devil are: Anyone who does not do what is right is not a child of God; nor is anyone who does not love his brother."*

> "Become the love
> you seek from a person,
> and that person will desire to
> be loving because of you."
>
> — Charles Rivers

Anyone that has attained any one of the three levels of universal love should move cautiously to the next. These levels of love are growth levels and not multiple chess moves. Anything beyond Eros (sexual) love will not be achieved by either manipulation or planned scheduling of your behaviors. One should not try to skip from Eros (sexual) love to Agape because they will surely face disappointment in such a venture. There is a learning process that takes place within the person who chooses the path to love another over simple love of self. In my own relationship it took an enjoyable and at times testy learning progression of some years for my wife and I to transition from an Eros (sexual) relationship to a Philia (friendship) love. It would take us another two years beyond that to achieve true understanding through Agape (true) love once we made the joint decision to be authentic with one other. So give your relationship and your spouse time to grow and remember what I told you: there is no challenge in loving someone who loves you back.

As we freely accepted our mother's love as children, surely we can freely give it away to our spouses, who may be love-challenged at this point in their life; and heavily burdened by the baggage of youth. Understand that there are other forces that you will face to challenge your relationship that at times will be undetectable. The bible tells us in Ephesians 6:12, *"For our struggle is not against flesh and blood, but against the rulers, against the authorities, against the powers of this dark world and against the spiritual forces of evil in the heavenly realms."* As a couple, know that long before Satan separated (husband) Adam and (wife) Eve from God, he separated (wife) Eve from (husband) Adam. In effect he was the first being ever to break one of the Creators edicts passed down from heaven. *"What therefore God has joined together, let no one set apart"* Matthew 19:6. In fact if the dark one ever attacks your home it will be in the same tempting patterns he used on Adam and eve.

Love is not conceited; it is not rude and does not act unbecoming. Love does not insist on it's own rights or it's own way. For it is not self seeking; it is not touchy or fretful or resentful.

1 Corinthians 13:5

*"To be controlling of others
one must first suspend his
or her own freedoms."*

— *Charles Rivers*

Surrender Your Need to Control

One of the colossal issues that couples face in their everyday home life is not a financial one or a sexual nature, as is played out in the popular culture. Couples' largest problems stem from control of one another, a tug of wills over who will be in charge of the home. In a home that is out of loves will a husband may try to control the relationship by sheer force while the wife may well try to control it through manipulation. Neither of these negative means used to achieve positive outcomes are the will of God. The Apostle Paul messengers a letter from prison by Tychicus to the church of Ephesus stating, *"That man is the head of the wife as Christ is the head of the church."*

That being said, I have had a field day instructing husbands who have misinterpreted the influence God has placed in them to guide their family's growth successfully. In my relationship classes I teach husbands and wives how the family of God knits together well by organization, humbleness and agreement. For the one who abides in God's sovereignty without submitting to authority draws condemnation and correction to their person. So if you wish to live your entire married life without true happiness, then rebellion is definitely the way to get on God's bad side. If your relationship is not working for you, then the Creator of love word is welcome in your home up to a limit. In this book entitled *Domestic Baggage*, I am going to give you an idea about how to change your relationship to where it calls down great favor, mercy and the blessings of the universe.

In Genesis 3:16, Eve is told that, *"Thy desire shall be for your husband and he shall rule over you."* Understanding the proper application of the word [rule] helps to diminish arguments as well as conflicting philosophies in your home. The definition of rule in a relationship is meant for governance and not control or domination. Let us analyze this further, for this definition has a much broader picture of governing. All of us citizens of the United States are under the rule or governance of someone or some organization, but ultimately God. If, as a man, you could take a hold of this reading, you could dramatically change the tempo of your relationship with your wife overnight.

As men and women citizens of varying countries, we exist under our government's rule. The design of some countries' constitutions is such that the rule is unobtrusive. Laws given to maintain peace and order will not concern you unless you do not follow their governance. Now on the other hand, some foreign rights abusive type governments have authoritative structures in which they are very obtrusive on the citizens' freedoms. In these countries not only do the leaders suspend several of the citizens' basic freedoms, but they restrict access outside of the country, making it a virtual prison for all but members of the government.

> *"If one makes arbitrary rules on their relationship, they slowly transition from spouse to cop in monitoring and policing of those sets of laws."*
>
> — Charles Rivers

Dictatorially privileged leaders of government end up becoming wardens of a prison of their own creation. In an attempt to crush their citizens' freedoms they have severely restricted their own. In all situations where you imprison freedom, the citizens will ultimately rebel. This situation is the same whether we are referring to a country, a city or your personal home. Even the hardest-hearted men who insist on reconstructing God's meaning for rule believes in free unfettered will for himself. He understands that people from all oppressed nations run, paddle or fly to free countries to be free under a more respective rule.

Now I am not suggesting for one minute that God meant for your home to be run like an autonomous governmental body, but he also did not mean to grant our wives free will for us to imprison it. When husband and wife place arbitrary rules on one another, they end up exchanging freedoms that keep their personal free will in check for the duration of that loveless relationship.

The Damaging Effects of Exchanging Freedoms

I was asked recently by an associate, who is an art dealer, why the husbands seemed to disagree with their wives on the choice of paintings that browsed about the collection. She was very much interested in making a sale on an oil painting in excess of $5,000.00 dollars when she realized her biggest hurdle to closing the deal was this one woman's spouse.

The very last thing she wanted to see was a husband back peddling over a negotiation she thought was firm with the wife. This art dealer was also miffed why some of the wives who shopped alone insisted that they would like to have their husband's opinions before making a purchase. Since this art dealer had been wounded by the institution of marriage through divorce she believed these wives should buy what they wanted regardless of what their husbands thought. I could understand her point of view if I analyzed relationship issues from a position of bad experiences or the preference of my gender over the other.

But I told her that I could show her what she could not see if she would allow me. Once she agreed, I told her it would have been better if those wives mentioned to their husbands that they hated a particular painting that they actually enjoyed. Why, then their husbands would have been sure to sway his opinion to like and purchase it. She said, "I never looked at it that way before." She took notice after that moment how in every disagreeable relationship in her showroom followed one spouse choosing something because it was the opposite of their spouse's wishes or demeanor.

I further explained to her that the reason those wives needed their husbands' permission was because somewhere down the line in their marriage history she restricted either his purchase ability or an idea that was near and dear to his heart. Now when it comes to something important to her, he is exercising his veto power of her decisions in a shared house. Examples of this are where one spouse tells the other I expect you back in two hours during a separate outing. Now the spouse that has made this rule has to go by their own policy when out and about as to not seem like a hypocrite. They end up not controlling their spouse as their original intent, but themselves.

Most anyone spiritual or otherwise can attest to the fact that God is the same unchanging God from Genesis through Revelations. His word is permanent and

God Throws Adam a Curve Ball

lives with us each day. We know that God's word is eternal for we are told, *"God is not a man that he should lie, nor a son of man that he should change his mind" Numbers 23:19* If you can agree on this much you should also know that when he gave Adam the gift of free will it was also extended to Eve forthwith after creation. The gift of free will has never been rescinded from mankind even to this day.

God did not say, "Adam, I will give thee free will — but Eve I will not!" Just as Adam, all women have the freedom to choose right or wrong in the sight of the Creator. God does not have humankind on puppet strings for he gave us both free will as opposed to guarded will. Add this gift to the mix of a home where the male is supposed to be the head of the wife and you can get for yourself some very interesting comic filled moments.

God believes in free will. You will find that when it is stated that a wife should either be subject or be submissive to her husband it is a request and not a demand. In Ephesians 5:21 wives are asked to, *"Be subject to your husband as (a service) to the lord."* But if you read further in Ephesians 5:25 husbands are asked to, *"love your wives as Christ loved the church and gave himself up for her."* This is sacrificing not as in just a job for income for your physical health and wealth. But also the life that made you an individual, our selfish lives as single men (*and gave himself up for her.*)

Some of the religious shout down other people In the faith who have one foot in spiritual life and the other in the world as being hypocrites. But I say to you that Jesus instructs us that the covenant of marriage is in itself a church. So if we have one foot in marriage and the other in our past single life of selfishness, does this not make us hypocrites to that institution?

If a church is doing wrong in teachings, its members (*children and family*) will fall away from it. If the Institution of marriage is not doing right in its teachings not only will it lose the members (children and family) but it will serve to scare others away from being converts to such love. Today we find that if people are not satisfied with their marriage they will exchange it just as easily as one picks up and leaves one church for another.

Ephesians 5:21 frames the entire institution of marriage between husband and wife. The bible never insists that a wife do something solely that it does not direct the husband to graciously mirror. A wife should submit to her husband just as clearly as man should submit his authority to Christ. If a man is not willing to submit authority to Christ, he should not expect his wife to submit to his authority.

> *"Never expect anyone*
> *to do something that you*
> *are not willing to do*
> *first yourself."*
>
> — *1SG. Louise A. Montero*

Look now at a similar example given in Colossians chapter 3 verses 18-21. It begins with instruction to wives, *"Wives be subject to your husbands, as is right and fitting and your proper duty in the Lord."* *19. Husbands, love your wives and do not be harsh or bitter or resentful toward them.* Finally the behavioral role of the children in a Christian home is identified. *20 Children, obey your parents in everything, for this is pleasing to the lord.* Note the only command given was to the child of the home as in [children, obey]. Never is it suggested that the wife obey the husband as a child would a parent.

In describing the family's harmony, He instructs the relationship of the father to the children. *21. Fathers, do not provoke or irritate or fret your children, lest they become discouraged.* In other words, do not break their spirit. So as men we must remember that if we are bitter with our wives we deny them the very same choices one enjoys most in freedom. That choice is to follow freely in humbleness as he instructs men and everyone in the body of his sovereignty. If we provoke our children, we risk making them wayward in the negatives we seek to keep them safe from.

In 1 Peter 2:13 all of us are instructed to, *"Be submissive to every human institution and authority for the sake of the Lord, whether it be to the emperor as supreme."* Now how many men could admit without flaw that they had, successfully submitted without question to the will of all of our governing authorities? As men we must honor our wives' submission as a gift and not a right of passage in order to be blessed by it. To receive this precious gift as a husband, you must yourself come under authority. For only under God's authority will you do right in your dealings and communications with your family. Otherwise, if we seek to draw authority from any place else but God, where must that authority originate?

> *"For the rebellious person swims against the tide of their own God given compassions."*
>
> — *Charles Rivers*

The Strength of Agreement, the Weakness of Rebellion

This chapter is written specifically to wives who have been struggling with submitting to their husbands in love. It was my ardent desire to include both roles of husband and wife as this caused the biggest fights in most couples that sought my help. Couples who did not claim to be spiritual did not seem to have as much as a problem as they chose in some cases to accept what was currently the standard. But I encourage women who insist on having Godly homes not to fight your husbands on every suggestion they offer, particularly when he is living correctly in the governance of his home as directed by God. This behavior serves little more than to de-convert you and your spouse and to cause your behavior to become as demonic as the husband who would lead his home as a dictator. Husbands who seek to depart a marriage through divorce usually report a sense of being unwelcomed by their family prior to their departure from the marriage.

This does not mean that his family actually told him that they did not need him, but in his opinion they never showed him that his presence served any purpose outside of being an annoyance. This feeling of being unwelcomed must dominate the air in a home, job or neighborhood before any man or woman flees it in order to save their spirit. This attitude of "I can do without you" is little more than rebellion of true love disguised as opposite gendered strife. Because God has placed husbands in this position of authority by draft instead of choice, you end up not fighting your spouse as much as you are fighting God. Because of this type of behavior, God will not bless your home any more than you would reward your children for their rebellious behavior.

Rebellion always brings with it a call down to correction while humbleness commands you to give favor to the respectful. But the way society behaves, you would have thought it would serve you to do the reverse. If one wishes to find out where you are failing in life or love, determine who or what you are rebellious towards. It may be your job, marriage or any place where you should have influence but you do not. People have a natural resistance to the spirit of rebellion.

If you discover an area in your life where you are prosperous and communicate well, you will find that you neither have rebellion nor resistance in that location. Take the behaviors that you apply to your successes and exhibit them In the areas in life you are deficient in and you will find yourself highly successful in a very short time.

When a wife rebels against her husband she must ask herself if she is rebelling against him or the fact that he is male alone. Does her rebellion stem from past relationships with the opposite gender or negative messages concerning them? Unless you forgive those men that may have hurt you and yourself for having a harmful opinion, you will destroy your own happiness. I have discovered that rebellion in the long run only affects the rebellious person. Because ultimately love always pays off with love and hate with hate in spades. People who have a rebellious nature at home, on the job, or in society don't get promoted or trusted. They cannot be trusted to promote because they will not complete anything that was asked of them by the person in authority over them without discussion, bitterness or apathy.

It is impossible for the hardened of heart rebellious person to learn because the rebellious person shuts his/her ear off to influence outside of their comfort zone. A wife who openly rebels against the influence of her husband unknowingly teaches her children to rebel against all authority. Ultimately those same children will rebel against their own mother as she remains the final authority over them. That same rebellious child cannot climb any ladder of success for they will be stopped by all those in authority over their growing years.

In Ephesians 4:1, it states, "*I therefore, the prisoner for the Lord, appeal to and beg you to walk (lead a life) worthy of the (divine) calling to which you have been called (with behavior that is a credit to the summons to God's service living as becomes you) with complete lowliness of mind (humility) and meekness (unselfishness, gentleness, mildness), with patience, bearing with one another and making allowances because you love one another.*"

Have you ever noticed how law enforcement identifies the rebellious person out of a group of people who are not? Yes, rebellion always calls down correction wherever it raises its head. Have you ever seen a rebellious child being removed from a classroom at school amidst a bunch of calm children who want to learn? The bible describes, in many different forms, the rewards of the humble compared to that of the rebellious. In 1 Peter 5:5 we are told, "*For God sets Himself against the proud [and He opposes, frustrates, and defeats them], but gives grace (favor, blessing) to the humble.*" In Luke 18:14, we are told, "*for everyone who exalts himself will be humbled, but he who humbles himself will be exalted.*" Lastly in Psalm147:6, we are told, "*The Lord lifts up the humble and downtrodden; He casts the wicked down to the ground.*"

Rebellion is one of the greatest tools in Satan's arsenal to undermine those who seek true love. In rebellion the dark one seeks to lift humans up against God, as he did himself, which ultimately brings the wrath of God down upon a person. The dark one was the first to convince man that they did not need God or his creation of marriage. He sought to convince Eve that she and Adam would be gods if they ate the fruit of rebellion, to loves will. That is precisely why God gave Adam and Eve the order of marriage authority just prior to expelling them from the Garden of Eden. Not only did Adam and Eve not become gods like they thought but their position in life

69

became lowered instead of raised for listening to The Dark One's demonic advice.

Why Divorces in True Love Equal those of Sexual Love

Although the physical and social manifestations of Agape love are the optimal goals of all couples and people on earth it becomes dangerous if left un-checked by simple friendship love. What I am bout to reveal to you alone is worth the pur-chase of this book by itself. Be-yond every factor that I have revealed to you so far as the destruction of the human relationship actual true love is among them.

Within the marriage or family dynamic more people head to divorce or separation on both ends of the spectrum at an equal rate by Agape love as they do over Eros love. The next thing a lot of them are starting to do is become friends after the divorce. I know I have told you up to this point that Agape love is your ultimate goal, and it is. But there is a danger in all homes whether the home is spiritual, secular or agnostic. Be-cause in all cases family love in and of itself represents Agape love, which makes it true love. But it is what happens in the natural environment of true love chemically. Once you place it behind closed doors at home that drives people to flee from family love. Have you ever noticed how you can get along with literally anyone outside of your home, but when you cross your doors threshold in the afternoon you feel conflict before it is even manifested? What about correcting your spouse on every decision they make as being in error to yours.

Why does true love hurt so much this way? Because every

level of love God gives us must be buffeted by another lesser or greater love in order to keep it from failing. We are spiritual mental and yet physical beings at the same time. Therefore we can not place ourselves as rigid in any one of these gifts of love without the flexibility of transitioning immediately to another as the relationship shifts.

A person who has only Eros (sexual) love for his partner will kill Philia (friendship) love and Agape (true) love in that relationship. Anyone who has only friendship love for their spouse will ultimately kill their sexual desire for that person. They can never truly have Agape love because they dishonor the physical love as something dirty or unnecessary. Finally an individual who has only Agape love and reaches only for God will end up with an Eros starved spouse who they can not be a friend to because they are not meeting their needs sexually.

In all families Agape (true) love conflicts will occur where there is not strong Philia (friendship) love. Why? Because in the family environment where true love exist it seeks to kill false love. False love is the basis for all disagreements within a family or coupled unit. True love requires that something wrong, hurtful or deceitful be purged from the relationship. This is different from the familiarity you have with the general public in your neighborhood or coworkers on your job.

Because once anyone of us steps outside of our front door we exist in an environment buffeted by either friendship love or false love. This is why someone who dislikes their home life can step outside and have nothing but smiles and waves for our neighbors and friends. The chemistry of true love behind closed doors can be stifling to dictatorship unless you remember to . . .

    a. Let your spouse make the same mistakes you would allow a friend.

b. Give an attentive ear to your spouse as you would a dear friend.

c. Allow yourself, your spouse and your children to experience laughter as you would enjoy in the presence of your closest unguarded friendship relationship

Develop a Hands-On Relationship

The longest journey most of us will ever take is the road leading back to finding true love. Witness on the streets a newly coupled man and woman and you will find two people so close to one another you would have believed that they were joined together at the hip. Men in these romantic early stages of the relationship massage their wives' feet until she feels most relaxed. Women in this same inspired state of early matrimony massage their men's scalps until they fall asleep in their arms like little children. Both sexes joyfully cook for one another and serve the meals in a loving way reminiscent of five star restaurants. Baths are drawn to candle lit music and rose petals are sprinkled from the tub to the bedroom of love making.

This is the essence of love, although an Eros relationship to start this behavior is what initially binds men and women together. When we do these types of loving actions we send our mates the message that we care for them immensely. Conversely, when we stop doing these actions over time we send them the message that we could care less about what activates love within them. But all is not lost, even if your relationship is currently void of these behaviors. Because a lot of these gifts of love we give are not authentic to our Eros love nature. They are merely copied from romantic films, magazines and suggestions from the world around us as the basis for what we lack in true love. So when we perform duties that are not authentic to our own true behaviors, over time they will fall away from our concern. To win back this type of personal touch relationship all one has to do is grow to the Agape love level. In this state of being a man gives a gift to his wife out of love, not out of service. A wife freely reciprocates not because she has to, but because there is a wanting desire to.

Now it is much easier to do all of these loving gestures and have them be natural to your nature — if you adopt God's meaning of love over yours. You see, God is the original inventor of love, romance and compassion. Did

The First Romance Was Orchestrated In Heaven

God the Father not make the Garden of Eden? I don't know about you, but there could not be a better place to be a natural romantic then in that type of setting. Did God the Father not present Eve to Adam? What a beautiful gift of romance to crown a Garden filled with love: a beautiful woman to share the rest of your life with. Yes, long before any romantic novel, magazine or television show, God was in the business of romance. Most men that I spoke with who had a problem connecting with their wives one on one had, over time, became estranged from her true love nature. A vast majority of the women who were married to their husbands for some period of time were still puzzled by his wants and desires of his heart. I recall one man who paid me a visit, puzzled about his wife's behaviors and desires, and saying, "I don't know what women want. I mean, should I just go out and get my wife roses?" I asked this particular husband how has his wife responded in the past when he has shown up at the door with a surprise of roses. The reply back from this man was, "Well she just put them in a vase until they died — as if she didn't care."

I then suggested he stop bringing home the roses and give her what she really wants. "What in the world would that be?" he said. I told him that after fifteen years of marriage, no one on earth should know her as much as he should. I told him that if he would just use the five senses that God gave him with his heart instead of his brain, he would know his wife. He said, "I'm willing to play, but I'm telling you that woman is a mystery."

I bet him that he could crack that mystery in a couple of minutes where years had left him puzzled about her behaviors. To prove this, I gave him a simple, practical exercise right then and there. I had him sit quietly and restful in a chair before me. Then I asked him to picture the contents on the bedroom dresser they had shared for the past fifteen years. He soon had a mental picture of what I wanted his mind's eye to see. I then told him to reach out and mentally place his hand on the smallest most replenishable item that she enjoys upon the face of that dresser.

In less than five seconds he shouted out, "She likes skittles candy!" I told him that this was just the smallest of successes that he would have the ability to taste if he stopped viewing his wife as one dimensional. It is important to all people, be they religious or non-religious, to understand that they are not married to all women or all men. Don't generalize your focus when it needs to be narrowed, as the husband found out when it came to his wife's favorite candy. For when your mind is on the entire world one could easily lose their car keys for an entire day only to find them later in your pocket.

Our five senses are utilized at each level of love from Eros (sexual) to Agape (true) love. Most people out of touch with the last two levels of love lean more upon the sexual cues of the first. In an Eros (sexual) relationship where there is sexual contact we use libido heightened sexual senses of hearing, sight, touching, taste and smelling. But this is not the finest

Fine-tuning the Five Senses of Love

that love has to offer; in fact, it is the very least that love can hope to offer up through the senses. Shortly after the act of sexual love making is over and erotic feelings have subsided, all five of these senses can dip to a less than nonchalant attitude between the participants. A couple that can be in tune in sex may not hear, see, touch, taste through physical contact anymore then sensing one another through smell afterwards.

Not one of the three spiritual levels of love God created operates as it should without the five senses being active. The only difference is that for each level of love you climb to, your senses grow from narrow-minded to spirit-minded. If you want to graduate your senses beyond the erotic level to the Philia level of communication you must master hearing your spouse as the person they are beyond the someone you wish they had become. If you can grow to accomplish this you will be able to physically touch them without having them withdraw from you. They will invite you into their world to taste how they see life. Your senses will become heightened to smelling out pleasures or troubles in your relationship.

At the highest level of the senses, Agape (true) love,

your closeness will be akin to standing in the presence of God with spiritual knowledge of your spouse. As a spouse you would have attained the *hearing* of the soul of the person you share a covenant with. You will have achieved the *sight* of God when it comes to viewing your spouse as one of His beautiful creations, regardless of if they are in a good mood or unpleasant one. You will have the God-given influence to *touch* their life and expand their influence as you never did before. As an Agape (true love) couple you will be able to *smell* the victory God intends for you long before it is visually manifested with tangible evidence. Most importantly, you will be able to *taste* the victories denied to you when you were in the infancy of love or an Eros (sexual) relationship.

Learning To Listen With the Spirit

The only way two friends anywhere on planet earth associate with one another is by listening with the heart (spirit) by way of their ears. If you communicate with anyone focusing merely on their auditory skills in association with the brain, your message will be lost in translation. For when communication is meant solely for the brain the listener engages the ability to filter out messages from the speaker. Listening other than with the heart (the souls center) is done primarily in school settings. Even in those settings if the teacher cannot grab the children's attention they risk a wave of tired eyes staring right back at them. If you have ever learned from a teacher in any level of schooling then that person touched your heart through your ears.

To listen by the spirit is to equate someone's present experience with your past experience of a similar occasion until you are present in the moment with them. This is the best way to empathize with another beyond the traditional barriers of opposite gender communications. Not by cutting them off to go over what you went through but by remembering the feeling you contract from their experience for a time. Most friends in communication have this talent down as fluid as breathing. I can vividly remember sitting with wives who tell me their husbands are bored with issues that concern them. But these same men assemble and listen to their friends for hours on end about the features of a new fishing rod with fast, alluring bait.

I have sat in conferences with husbands who admitted that their wives could care less about the real issues that cause them anxiety. On the other hand, these women pay attention for weeks at a time about their girlfriends' trials and suspicions concerning their boyfriends. If husband and wife learn to listen through the ears to the heart (spirit), you can cross gender barriers of association. Did you know that some of the best salespeople in the country communicate with you this way? It matters not that the product is a car, groceries or drugs peddled by a street junkie. The salesperson If proficient at their craft bypasses your ears and goes straight for the heart. If they are good salespeople they will supply the needs of your heart. If they are bad salespersons they will only manipulate you to make a quota to attain wealth.

Now if you ever came upon a salesperson who could not connect with you it was because they were trying to sell your mind through facts concerning the product. They had not attained seasoning for the position they held, just as a young husband or wife falls short in communicating. In Matthew 6:21, it says, *"For where your treasure is, there will your heart be also."* Does your spouse have your heart when he or she communicates; and if not, who does?

Learn to Stay Calm in a Stressed Situation

It is written that the enemy (Satan) comes to kill, steal and destroy. But usually by the time we have learned to recognize his footprints he has accomplished his dirty work and is well on the retreat. The tools Satan uses to get in your home are the same he has been using since the beginning of time: namely our anger, discord and strife in that order.

Did you know that the average person provides safety for themselves by driving with a seat belt on? Once the vehicle is parked at home they lock the doors and set the car alarm. Inside of the home they feel safe behind strong doors and double locks from burglars. Beyond these protections they set motion alarms prior to going to bed. Should a burglar get beyond all of these security measures, he will have to contend with the loaded weapon for protection in the night-stand drawer. Surely we feel safe, but it is a false sense of security.

For you see the most dangerous burglar has the ability to sneak into our homes and take all your possessions. He is not content with just stealing all of our hard earned possessions, but our life force as well. That criminal is the devil and he easily bypasses all of man's protective measures. Why? Because once we feel safe we leave the doors of our mind and spirit wide open to attack. We disarm the security and put away our weapons (spiritual discernment). Eliminate the devil's ability to invade your home through your mind and you are well on your way to evicting him from your recovering marriage. If you want to know if the devil is in your relationship conflicts then apply this principle. Take the "d" off of the word devil and see if evil happenings are building In ever increasing intensity all around you.

No matter whether we are talking about cars on a busy roadway, boats on a crowded lake, or couples in an aggravated situation, when two objects meet each other without any clear authority on how to yield, a collision will occur. Each time

How to Avoid a Collision of Opinions

we argue with our loved ones we are trying to hold our ground on our personal reasoning. This is the chemistry for all disagreements: we only fight for our right of way and refuse to acknowledge the other person's right to an opinion. Cars use traffic to yield, boats use right of ways. For humans, the clear yield sign in any conflict is respect of the persons right to be heard.

If you lack respect, you will only hear your own opinion bouncing off of the person you are drowning out. We respect our outside of the home friends' opinions when they are wise or when it is otherwise. We even side with them if they have a better opinion then ours. Couples who have lost respect for one another and refuse to yield in a discussion come to relationship conferences, counselors and therapist to have them play traffic cop. It becomes the job of the counselor to stand guard over a broken interchange signal and ensure that husband and wife yield respectfully at the communication traffic intersections. But playing cop to two aggressive conversationalist drivers is never a permanent solution to disrespect in a marriage.

So instead in my classes and seminars I have each spouse become conscious of the root cause of their behavior so they can change it. When I have a couple where the husband or wife exclaims they hate their spouse, I show them how this estranges them from their own spiritual essence. For when we hate our spouses we not only work in opposition to true love but against our own humanity. To understand how, you must first understand the statement, "I hate my husband." A wife reveals her true un-Godly nature when she says *I hate*. It truly does not matter whether this person placed the words *my husband* at the end of that declaration or something else. The declaration of the spirit has come through the mouth of the messenger.

When we profess hurtful statements like these we reveal our true painful nature that is masked by our pleasant demeanor. No one can be all loving and yet all hating at the same time; that person will live in constant conflict inside of themselves. Usually when we get angry at our spouse it is not because of what they have done but because of what has been done to us prior to marrying them. Our anger grows from a small spark inside that, if left unchecked, grows into a raging flame. That spark may begin with just a fleeting comment from another person in your work environment. Combine work stress with a two hour traffic jam and you will be primed for a prickly nature.

Why are we so susceptible to anger from others? Because human nature is geared in such a way that we become sponges to the environment we inhabit. If we spend an entire day in a pleasant, loving environment, we absorb that love and come home with the ability to squeeze out that level of love. But if we have occupied a negative, energy-draining environment, we come home and wring out all of that pain over our personal relationships and ourselves.

Once we arrive home and get into a difference of opinion with our spouse it will begin with a testy *thought*. "I can't believe you said that to me," goes off in your head. The mind now grows in anger as we come into what I call *inthoughtsified behavior*. This means even after your differ- ence of opinion has passed you continue to stew internally. "Why would he say that to me? Look at all I have done for him! Why I was with that man when no one even cared." These thoughts leave two once loving adults sleeping in two separate rooms and ignoring one another for days on end.

While resting in separate spaces without resolution you transition to the last stage I call *inthoughtsification*. You are now drunk with thoughts of what if, why would, and maybe ifs. Your mind begins to run overtime, even during sleep — if you can manage to squeeze in any. Work now takes on a whole new meaning as it becomes your respite from your spouse, whom you should have been able to lean upon for friendship and support. Both husband and wife are waiting for apologies from the other for something that did not originate from the marriage. We cannot expect our home relationships to remove what the outside world conveys upon our spirit on a daily ba- sis. When you are inthoughtsicated you must break your focus by realizing you are drunk with thoughts of indifference.

In your current state of indifference, the devil has craftily gained a foothold in your home and, if you are not careful, for the rest of your life. He has slid in the front door of your sanctified home where even salesman is barred entrance. He has infiltrated your mind with frustration and thoughts of anger. In this aggravated state not only is the devil winning against love in your sanctified home, but at this level of an- ger you would, on a whim, trade your entire future finances, family and happiness in hopes of being single again. The enemy comes to steal, kill and destroy because divorce is such a permanent fix for a temporary problem.

Saturate Your Sponge Before You Go to Work

To head off office, commute or personal inner dialogue that fills the sponge of indifference to capacity you must start your day on the right foot. Did you know that a sponge that is already completely saturated cannot be filled by another drop of water? So goes the same for your mind and spirit. Both must be nurtured in the morning just as well as your body to stay in a right frame of mind. When you roll out of bed in the morning before you get a bite to eat or start you're athletic regimen ensure you take time out to meditate spiritually in a way that sends you out the front door with a more spiritually discerning heart and a positive countenance.

By doing this you will find that far fewer things will have a hold on your existence as they once did. People will still try to saturate your sponge but with daily persistence on your part that negative water will roll off the back of you're already saturated positive spirit. People will not only tell you that you have changed who you are, but they will change who they are around you. Take heed though and do not get comfortable with your new found stress regulating success. For just as someone who stops exercising you will loose strength in this area until your resistance becomes weakened to the state it once rested in.

*"Iron sharpens iron; so a man
sharpens the countenance of his friend,
[to show rage worthy purpose].*

— Proverbs 27:17

During an apprehensive private relationship class I listened as a husband requested that his wife be more of a mother and a happier wife to him. His wife, seated across the table from him, wanted her husband to be more relaxed and intuitive to her feelings. I find it funny how the universe matches opposites to live with one another in marriage. This leaves couples in a quandary: husband and wife find themselves asking their spouse for something they feel completely incapable of doing.

When Bringing Out the Worst *In* You is Best *For* You

This does not mean that they won't be able to do them at some future date, but they are currently resistant to change in this area. But if we yield out of respect to our spouses we could let go of the negatives in our life and we would be capable of concurring not only on things that our spouse does not particularly like in us but what we feel is intolerable within ourselves.

This is the entire majesty of the Creator of the universe; he always places opposite strengths together to sharpen one another's weakness into newfound relational vigor. We are called as spiritual lovers to draw out the bitter portions of one another and replace them with love. Marriage draws out the truths in people that no other relationship is willing to address. Why even your own outside of the home friends will tolerate and adjust to your negative behavior as much as they will your positive. That type of blind understanding will never bring you to change but just further estrangement to true love.

In fact, the wrong that our friends tolerate in us is no

more than twofold behavior. If our friends caught their spouse doing what they tolerate in us they would be absolutely up in arms. I had a session with a wife who was extremely angry at her husband when she had little more than a belief that he had committed adultery on her. But oddly enough, she remained best friends with another woman who she had knowledge of adulterous affairs for over seven years on her husband. Once I pulled this information from her she decided to get rid of that friend. One thing the Creator of the universe will allow what ever you condone to be revisited upon your front door.

Our View unto the World

Staying calm in the midst of an edgy discussion will yield the most precious relationship gold imaginable. On the rainiest, coldest day of the year, when people prefer to be warm inside, someone is found splashing in puddles without a coat or a care in the world. To us, maybe yesterday was considered the worst day of our life while someone in another part of the country was celebrating the birth of a newborn. Down the block from you, God has just answered a lifetime prayer for one of your neighbors. What we see and feel inside becomes our version of reality.

This is why, when in a tense discussion with your spouse, you should expect him or her to see a different reality from the same conversation based on the current mood. If you do not listen to your spouse in a disagreement, what is missed will be revisited in subsequent arguments in louder tones. As a couple you must take that rebellious nature out of your relationship in order to merge as a team. The rebellious nature is such that it prevents the forming of any team before it is removed from a person or an environment. My experience in the military basic training camp is that they accept young people from all backgrounds from different parts of the country.

Now the drill instructors use basic training for one purpose mainly. They know that most of these children just left their parents' home where they openly rebelled against all authority. This means that they are the last people on earth who can make a cohesive team. The rebellious nature must be removed in order to merge them into a team of soldiers. What remains is self control, respect for the team effort and newfound honor for the parents they originally disobeyed. A large percentage of people who could not make it through basic training were never team players. So whether you are in the military, on the job, or married, you must be willing to learn the essence of a team.

"Those who
make themselves
receptive to the needs of
their spouse become in their
actions most desirous."

— Charles Rivers

In relationships we are attracted to our spouses, in many cases, because their persona is contradictory to our own behavior. I strongly believe we are attracted to what we once found beautiful within our own

Thank God We're Different

nature at one time, but is now missing or hidden. An uninteresting man will find himself gravitating to a free-spirited woman. Why, because he once was a free-spirited boy before he went through the trials and distractions of youth. So, in essence, he is attracted to what is best but now dormant within himself, which is the core of healing in the relationship of merging to free willed spirits.

A woman who has no organizational skills finds herself strangely attracted to a man who is insanely efficient and time focused. So we are attracted to our mates as opposites. In America, it is a well known fact that fifty percent of all first time marriages end in divorce. These marriages are mainly made up of opposite natured people. They become convinced that opposite character couplings are the death of marriage. As people enter their second marriage they tend to turn to people who are of the same nature. They set their course on a mistaken quest of harmony by finding a clone of themselves in the opposite gender.

Why are people motivated to do this? Because they are bombarded by radio, television and internet experts who seek to convince us that we should be compatible to achieve harmony in a relationship. But woe to those people who fall for this belief, because an astounding sixty-seven percent of all second marriages end in divorce and these are mainly made up of people who were looking for themselves. Current surveys gives us additional data that most third marriages have a seventy-six percent chance of divorce. As humans we are akin to poled magnets, attracted by the opposite and repelled by the same when it comes to choosing a spouse.

This is why you should honor your differences during a disagreement. Just because your spouse's opinions are not yours does not mean they are wrong. Our job as couples on the same team should be to find out how we can turn a disagreement into an agreement on common grounds. Since we are attracted to the opposite, what does your spouse's mannerisms, attitudes and work ethics say about you? Do they overshadow you, revealing weaknesses you did not know you had or do they fall far short, showing that you are too vocation focused?

Your differences should compliment one to another. Salt and sugar (men and women) make for good baking ingredients. But if the blend of one of the two is stronger it will spoil a good recipe; it will destroy a great marriage. Despite the belief that one's life will be much better living with someone of the same character, I believe differently. For it is the people who fought the hardest to convert their spouses who end up missing all of those little Idiosyncrasies that made them so different.

You see, the worst thing we can do is marry someone for a difference and then switch up and try to convert them from that difference. To arrive successfully at Agape (true) love for your spouse, others or God, you must end self love. What is self love? Certainly not the expression of a healthy love for yourself. This type of exclusive love occurs when you have no other love but for yourself. We are often told that "you cannot love someone else unless you first love yourself," but actually you cannot love someone else unless you first yield love of self.

Volunteer
to cater to your
spouse's needs and
desires of the heart without
any inhibition on your part. Seek to
understand through the healing
process their past pains and
tribulations of a once
wounded spirit.

Baggage Handler

"Those who learn to give of self
die to self, and broaden their
capacity to love another."

— *Charles Rivers*

I have found time and time again in my communications with couples that God sends pain specific spouses in the lives of those persons who need and want change. These pain-specific spouses have the unique ability of meeting their mates on whatever love

Volunteer Your Love for Life

89

level they have been wounded upon. Now that does not mean that these pain-specific spouses will come to you as angels.

As a matter of fact, they will usually come to the relationship with just as many concerns as you brought to the marriage. But in helping to heal their pains you will find your own easier to forgive. Unbeknownst to them, they are on a mission to free you of the pains you have absorbed or the unforgivingness you refuse to relinquish. At times, God even pairs up a set of people who can only heal one another through their opposite behavior struggle.

People Are Wounded By Love, Not By Hate.

If someone has been hurt in the world, it is do to love and not hate. Do you believe that? As humans, we are disappointed at the level that people let us down on the Eros, Philia or Agape levels of love. It is much easier for us to guard our heart against hate, but it is when hate sneaks in as love that we are powerless to defend ourselves. If you are young and dating someone and you find out that they have betrayed you by having sex with someone else, you will feel hurt by betrayal of Erotic (sexual) love. Being betrayed at the lowest level of love usually makes people cautious about the faithfulness of the opposite gender for their entire lives.

If, during your growing years, you have a friend who betrays your solemn trust, you would have been hurt by Philia love. In the future you will be cautious to letting your guard down too soon to new friends.

If you feel you have ever been hurt by your parents or God and you believe the event to be unforgivable, then you have been hurt by Agape (true) love. Since the love of family is created through God, having mistrust in this level of love will definitely delay an individual's true path to spiritual love. Some people who have had either a death in the family or a great financial fall in their lives feel that God may have betrayed them.

In exchange for what they perceive as loss of guaranteed love, they turn their backs in kind on spiritual love. They feel that God's love and protection should be guaranteed enough to prevent any tragedy from ever befalling their lives. This thinking is about as unrealistic as tragedies occurring within marriages being the fault of the unwitting participants. If God allows life to carry on where we go through the valley of death and emerge on the other side, in tact then that should tell us something. We should reciprocally allow our spouses the benefit of the doubt when things happen on their time that remains out of anyone's control?

There is truly a connection of blame that is the same in marriage as it is for God when it comes to expectations of failed miracles. In both relationships we can feel wounded or turned away by love permanently to the detriment of our own happiness. But it depends on what we do next that shows what type of love we are really made of in the presence of pain. If we allow ourselves to get angry immediately, as spirit filled people, then we reside in Eros (sexual) love. Eros (sexual) love in the body of the non-spiritual or the spiritual person has no patience for mistakes. But, if in the face of pain or betrayal we insist that there is a brighter day, we reside in the mindset of Philia (friendship) love. If you persist through the face of pain and discouragement in seeking the will of God at your worst moment In life, then you exist in the Agape (true) level of love.

*"Multiple layers of injury
necessitate multiple layers
of healing."*

— *Charles Rivers*

How Does One Redeem a Heart Once it has been Wounded by Love?

All of us who have been hurt by a particular level of love must be healed by that same level of love. One who has been hurt on the Agape level of love should not expect that an erotic (sexual) relationship will heal them. If you were hurt in a particular love, the universe usually will send you someone to assist your healing through that form of love. A person who has been sexually violated may be sent an Individual who has patience in these areas. These, what I refer to as pain-specific persons, will not rush your healing process, even if they are estranged to what has happened to you. But remember that each person that God sends to be part of your healing process has in themselves been given strength to stand only a limited test of their time and patience. These persons will outlast anyone else in your life that would flee you in times of trouble. But you will know when even you have pushed them too far. For when they do decide to leave, you would have gone beyond the limits of surrendering your past hurts and pains for love instead.

The first thing that most of us that have been wounded by love carry out is to get angry and frustrated at anyone and anything around us. This follows the feeling of mistrust and a resentful spirit towards those people who failed to love us properly. This does not mean that we will take retribution upon those persons who wronged us. But it will make future dealings painful for those who are close to reopening those wounds. To act in this manner, one must cast a blanket of blame against all persons from that same gender, ethnic or racial background. At this point we are choosing to consciously withhold love from others as it was withheld from us at that critical juncture. Once a person walls off their heart (gold) to others like Fort Knox no one will get the chance to witness your true beauty. For when we wall off what is best in us all we have left is the mind and the body. When we withhold God's love from people who are entitled to it, we steal something precious from them and the world.

> *"Volunteerism is the enemy*
> *of unforgivingness for it requires*
> *that we free ourselves from*
> *the protective trappings of*
> *self preservation."*
>
> *— Charles Rivers*

When we deny love to those closest to us, they will in turn do the same towards people they come in contact with. Such a ripple effect can take place that will ultimately kill a family, a community and the body of civility. The absence of love creates all conflicts. It depletes the air and suffocates the life out of your home. You cannot have a conflict at home any more than you could between two countries without the absence of love, God's love in us.

"We either bring
people our love or we
present them with our current
circumstances."

— *Charles Rivers*

During a bad state of mind, we withdraw love from a room just as surely as we bring love in with us in a positive mood. All of us bring one of the three loves wherever we roam. For instance, a young lady who wants to attract a young man flirtatiously sends out signals of Eros (romantic or sexual) love. That same young lady in the company of a girl friend sends out the signals of Philia (friendship or communicative) love. She can then turn her behavior and attitude towards spirituality to allow herself to feel Agape (true or spiritual) love.

Each day, just as surely as we can bring love to an environment, we can cancel out certain loves that exist within an environment. The Pope, or any highly recognizable religious figure can walk into any bar where there is drinking and swearing and immediately vanquish Eros (sexual) love from the room and fill it with Agape love before the lights were even turned up — that is not to say that they would ever visit any of these places.

"One who
finds it hard to
forgive another bases
their forgiveness upon merit.
They are estranged to true love
which offers all forgiveness
through grace.

— *Charles Rivers*

For countless marriages, it would seem as if the loneliest time in the participant's lives is spent in the presence of one another. Tina and John were just that type of troubled couple; their names are changed here

Learning How to Forgive

to give them anonymity. Tina arrived at my office frustrated, with grimace on her face that honestly went about as low as her chin. She sat for at least one hour into the session with her arms crossed defensively. She was mad and she wanted everyone in that room including her husband to know it. Her trust for her husband had left their relationship years ago. She revealed to me that she was sure that her husband had cheated on her. Because of this, she refused to have sexual intercourse with him and avoided any personal affection towards him for the last two years.

My personal mission regarding Tina's marriage would end up being threefold. To start, I would work on bringing stability to an already crumbling relationship. Secondly, I would turn the parents' focus off of selfish exploits and back towards their children who sorely missing it. Lastly, but more important than the other two, I would show Tina the meaning of forgiveness for past offenses. The last part would be even more difficult by the fact that she was still smarting from knowing that her parents divorced because her father had cheated on her mother when she was a teenager.

So, in Tina's mind, this just reaffirmed the comment she made about men being "that ninety-nine percent of them cheat around on their wives." I don't care what anyone says, adultery is a hard hurt for anyone to overcome it matters not if you are a man or woman. But I believe that all of the doctors and therapists, counselors included, that ever walked this

95

planet never gave us the tools to cope with this subject as much as Jesus Christ did in one act. If you are familiar with the bible, I am referring to the confrontation in which Mary Magdalene was being chased by the Scribes and Pharisees to be stoned to death for the then crime of adultery, *John 8:1-7*.

The assembled who planned to stone her figured that not only would they get the chance to kill Mary Magdalene but they could get Jesus if he agreed with her and broke the law given to Moses by God. The Scribes and Pharisees addressed Jesus concerning her case: did he believe she should be stoned to death? Hearing their question, Christ turned to write in the sand and then back to address them. Jesus said, "Yes I know and agree about the laws given Moses." He then told them that, "*he who is among you that is without sin let him be the first to cast a stone at her.*"

This comment, in my mind, ended the practice of stoning, for you see, one by one, the Scribes and Pharisees walked away, from the eldest to the youngest, because they were convicted by their own consciences. There have been some religious scholars that speculate what Christ wrote in the sand with his finger while briefly looking at each accuser was words like liar, thief, murderer just to mention a few of the commandments. They believe that he was sending a silent message to the men in his presence because he had the innate ability given to him by God to know their past.

The Pharisees may not have committed adultery, but all of them knew that they had broken one or all of God's Commandments. They knew because of this that they were the last people on earth to be able to question Mary Magdalene or anyone else for that matter. Christ then turned to Mary Magdalene to ask, "*Woman, where have your accusers gone?*" He knew that the Pharisees stood in as the jury and his job was to be the judge of this hastily assembled kangaroo court.

Mary responded to him, "*They have gone my Lord.*" Christ in turn replied to her, "*Then I can judge you neither, go and sin no more.*" You see the sin of adultery is just that, a sin. The sin of adultery carries no higher weight of condemnation than lying or stealing. For in Revelations 21:8 we are told, "*That even the liar will have his place in the lake of fire.*"

As an author to the institution of marriage, I carry no cavalier attitude towards the sin of adultery than I do any other. But I tell you this and it is the truth that any person, community or nation that holds Erotic (sexual) love higher than true love will find high crimes and misdemeanors in the sin of adultery. I explained this to Tina during our heated session. Adultery is one of the sins in the laws given the human race and not the most damning one. God does not rate the Ten Commandments as man chooses to.

He does not indicate any lenience towards lying while holding His ground on adultery. Knowing this, Tina could not stand in judgment of her husband anymore then those Scribes and Pharisees would be able to Mary Magdalene. For in Tina's lifetime she had surely broken most, if not all, of the Ten Commandments. Certainly she had taken God's name in vain within her lifetime.

Most undeniably, in her short lifetime she had stolen and bore false witness against another. She had admitted to coveting the house, careers and vehicles of her best friends. So in essence Tina found herself with a rock in her hand against Mary Magdalene (*her husband*). I explained to Tina that forgiveness is a gift where three win. In forgiving her husband she actually becomes the first person in her husbands' life outside of his mothers and Gods unconditional love to forgive

97

his selfish behaviors. Therefore her husband gets restored by receiving her true gift of love.

> *"One should only*
> *count themselves as*
> *healed who has first developed*
> *forgiveness in their heart towards*
> *the person they embrace the*
> *greatest animosity."*
>
> — *Charles Rivers*

Secondly, in her case, she actually gets to practice her love walk by forgiving her husband while in an other than pleasant state of mind. But third and just as important as the first God Himself benefits by her forgiveness. For we are told in Matthew 6:14 that, *"For if you forgive people their trespasses [their reckless and willful sins, leaving them, letting them go, and giving up resentment], your heavenly Father will also forgive you."* When we forgive those who have hurt against us we dismiss the wrath that they were ultimately supposed to face from Gods judgments for wronging us. In Romans 12:19, *"Dearly beloved, avenge not yourselves, but rather give place unto wrath: for it is written, Vengeance is mine; I will repay, saith the Lord."*

In her angered and embittered state, she has actually given of herself to her offender. This is Christ-like in nature to forgive another before they deserve it, and no higher love is there. As a bonus, Tina gives herself the gift of liberation: the liberation from hatred which had its hold on her very soul for a long time. Yes, three always benefit from the gift of forgiveness. To forgive is a gift to someone before they are worthy of it, just as God the Father forgives us before we are truly deserving of it.

He does not wait until we are deserving of the gift; if He did, we would never be able to achieve it.

Tina's original problem was that she had to forgive her father for the same offense before she could forgive her husband. She had held so long to her unforgiving state that it had become part of her makeup as a human being. The excess baggage we carry through life is a living testimony to God of our unwillingness to forgive and leave the past behind. Look into your past at the people who have wronged you. Make a mental list if you must, but start on your personal path of forgiveness today. Unforgivingness has hurt your past. It will damn your present and withdraw life right out of your future.

Judged as Angels

In the conference room where I regularly taught classes, I have projectile ceiling lamps that I stand under for a demonstration. It is a demonstration of the light we place our spouses in. When you see your spouse as some sort of angel over a human you deny them their humanity and human frailties. Of course all humans will falter; it is their fallen nature.

God knew that we were flawed since the initial fall of man. In life, most people will carry an "anything goes" attitude with their friends because they don't want to see them pigeon-held by any rules they would impose upon them. At the same time, we carry an angel-like appearance with our spouses that will not allow them their human frailties lest our full wrath be unleashed upon them.

So if we take it upon ourselves not to forgive our spouses for an offense we act outside of loves will. Once we deny our spouse the blessings of forgiveness God reciprocates our ingratitude in kind. For the Father will not bless any home that curses his will. Again in Matthew chapter 6:14 it states, *"For if you forgive people their trespasses (their reckless and willful sins, leaving them, letting them go, and giving up resentment), your heavenly Father will also forgive you. But if you do not forgive others their trespasses (their reckless and willful sins, leaving them letting them go, and giving up resentment), neither will your Father forgive you your trespasses."* One does not even have to await an after life to face the fate of unforgivingness. For we are told that if we do not forgive those that have wronged us we will be turned over to that which torments us seen and unseen in life until we do. Matthew 18:22-35

If one finds
their torment of
spirit they have identified
their purpose to
forgive

Why then is it easier for outside of the home friends to forgive and love in the Agape sense where it is difficult for couples? Primarily it is because same sexed friends have a leg up on their relationships. It is not because they are compatible by any stretch of the imagination. By definition of their relationship they completely bypass the first category of love being Eros (sexual) and proceed directly to the Philia (friendship) level of love.

Since most friends are of same sex they don't have to view one another as anything other than close friends first. So an outside of the home relationship starts on a higher plane to begin with. It begins on the level of love, communication, compassion and forgiveness. This also makes it easier for them to move towards an Agape (true) love level, which is only one stage higher than friendship love. The greatest difficulty of opposite gender relationships is that they are condemned to start at the lowest level of love and struggle to climb higher than just the base level of love. But in condemnation one finds beauty in the fact that anyone can grow to be loving from a loveless heart or erotic filled coupling if they allow themselves.

"Love takes no account of the evil done to it. It does not rejoice at injustice and unrighteousness, but rejoices when right and truth prevail. Love bears up under anything and everything that comes."

1 Corinthians 13:5-7

It is far easier to forgive than it is to hold onto a grudge. Most people would believe the contrary to be true but I will show you the error of that belief. Paul writes to the Ephesians *"Do not let the sun go down while you are still angry"* Ephesians 4:26. He knew that not only will your day be destroyed in an anger state but so would your night. In fact, if you went to bed in an anger state there is a good possibility that you would wake up the same come the next morning or possibly for the rest of your life.

Forgiveness and Its Positive Effects on Health

The indulgence of unforgivingness is the most costly and deadliest of all of the sins plaguing human beings. In its roots it is responsible for more internal diseases, conflicts and murders than anything else on the planet today. It causes you to sulk, turning down the corners of your mouth until you achieve permanent frown lines on your face. If you are a woman, there is not enough makeup or botox to reverse what the act of forgiveness does for those pesky frown lines. It causes an innumerable amount of skilled and unskilled workers to call in sick from work or quit their jobs because they cannot get along with their coworkers. It is the impetus for a family member to cease communication with his/her siblings for life.

Imagine the savings to our personal medical insurance if we could just learn how to forgive. It has been said that, "most people die not from what they eat, but what is eating at them. Picture the savings of being able to avoid expensive psychological or marriage counseling sessions. Visualize for yourself the eliminated visits to the hospital to treat symptoms of preventable diseases spurred on by bitterness and unforgivingness.

The medical community would lose billions of dollars annually if most of us searched our souls before searching for external cures to internal dialogue. I once remember giving advice to a woman who believed it was impossible for humans to forgive. I encouraged her to read Luke 1:37, *"That for with God nothing is ever impossible and no word from God shall be without power or impossible of fulfillment."* Any connoisseur of hope or motivation knows that you must believe with a positive mind or all else is lost before the journey begins. So again if we cannot see our way to doing an act that is kind, just or right, we are acting in our will and not in loves will. For most of us the biggest tug of war is between doing what love wants when we are happy and doing what we feel when we are angry or disenchanted.

Learning How to Forgive Your Parents

We have identified up to this point that some pains might have come about due to our upbringing. But I'm here to tell you that you can forgive your parents and clear their conscience and yours at the same time. Because a lot of the mistreatment, mistakes and hurt that your parents may have visited upon your person was not their original intention for marriage or children. I find myself teaching couples this truth all the time before I can ever assist them on their own relational problems. I awaken their senses about the true spirit of their parent's original intentions for life and love. I accomplish this by showing them that no infant is born to the intention of growing up and abusing or mistreating their own children.

No parent has a plan at the creation of their newborn of making a conscious effort to inflict pain of the mind, body or spirit that they could not bear themselves as children. They went through something painful themselves in their youth by fate or possibly by choice that changed their makeup as a loving individual in the presence of those who needed them most, namely their children. They believed later on in life, after getting married and having children, that they could keep those pains and frustrations in check. But that idea is fine on a perfect sunny day without any financial or personal problems. But the difficulty happens when they are under maximum pressure, for that is the same circumstances that the disease of bitterness or abuse was bequeathed unto them. Unforgivingness always manifests itself to destroy beautiful environments when people are generally stressed out. So in essence we end up not facing an angry person but a person who is unwilling to forgive someone or some thing.

Most of the couples who came to me with complaints about their parents also had children and I witnessed to the last a mirrored behavior of their upbringing. If the wife received pain as a child she issued it in kind to her child in the present. If a father went through something painful with his parents he put his children through the same. So even though these couples came to see me with complaints about their parents they were blind to the fact that they were doing the same thing to their children. I imagine that this is the same scenario that took place between their parents and them. It is true that *"whatever gets pressed down upon you becomes you unless you are willing to forgive the people who have offended you."* Forgiveness must be granted first post-occurrence or posthumously in order to break any painful cycle. Those that can successfully forgive end up breaking the cycle of hatred and unforgivingness with this generation of their family.

Learning How to Forgive Everyone Else

If you can learn to forgive your parents and your spouse than it should be a lesson of discovery to forgive anyone else. Not simply for the sake of forgiving but in the understanding of the human levels of love each one of us manifest. For the people that offend you currently only operate out of whatever level of love they have achieved in life thus far, just as you do. This is why the God judges the heart and not the words or exterior appearances of people. Peter writes in Acts 10:34 that *"Most certainly and thoroughly I now perceive and understand that God shows no partiality and is no respecter of persons."* If someone has not achieved any higher level than Eros (sexual) love for himself and society it will be a far stretch on your part to expect Agape (true) love from them.

Only God knows that the person who hurt you may have been hurt that way by someone else. For the bible tells us that *"Vengeance is mine sayeth the Lord."* His judgments will weigh out the truth of each persons individual spirit. But to reduce your level of love to a lower one in order to match the anger of an adversary only secures a very painful place for two people instead of one. We will be judged by God upon why did we not try to bring that person up from a lower love to a higher love.

*"The ultimate
test of forgiveness is in
people being able to release
themselves from a painful past that
they had no power over
to control."*

— Charles Rivers

More prominent in the minds of people who attend relationship enrichment courses beyond for- giveness of parents is forgiveness of self. A person must be brought to forgiveness of self before they can expunge destructive behaviors from their relationship. Most men and

Learning How to Forgive Yourself

women that I encourage to forgive themselves admitted to me that they did not have a personal problem or that they did not see any need to forgive themselves. This was completely untrue, for all people are changed by their upbringing and environment for the positive or the negative. Only some of our positive changes in our eyes could end up being positively negative in our spouses. Most people, wives or husbands, that . came to me complaining about their mates thought that they had not changed since childhood.

But I showed them a child starts at one level then re- ceives pains, unrequited pressures, and the like from the world. This takes their level of love and humanity down a few notches. Therefore they must be brought back up to that level before they feel a sense of resolution over guilt. I once revealed to a woman a sure fire test to see if you approve of who you have become as an adult apart from ignoring what you won't acknowledge. I told her only one person on earth can honestly stand in judgment of her.

She told me that she knew who judged her behavior, God right? I said, "For sure one day God will stand in judgment of her, but today for this task you can stand in judgment of yourself." I asked her to vividly think back to her earliest memory of younger days: when she had a more innocent demeanor and love for any and everyone. You too can practice this lesson as I explained it to her.

I told her even at that time she could feel if someone loving or was mean spirited simply by being in their presence. The loving person draws little children in with their demeanor and the people who are not true to themselves inside repel them away. In fact, in most children's neighborhoods there is always a house where they determine an older man or woman true or falsely to be the scary person. They avoid this house like the plague because of the person's attitude, even if a smiling face buffers that attitude. Children can run away from a smile just as quick as a frown if they think you are exhibiting other than your true nature.

So I asked her if she was ready to judge herself and her attitude. I told her to imagine for a moment that she could separate that little innocent child she once was from the adult she now is. Now if that little child came in this room right now and looked her in the face, what would she think? Would she be glad of what she had become or would she wish for something different? Would she see herself as that scary person on the block that she and her friends tried to avoid? Would she want to rush to her arms to be embraced by love or would she perceive an absence of true unadulterated love? No one can stand in better judgment of our behavior on earth than we can from the point of view of the innocent.

I have heard this statement bantered about often enough in confidence from topics ranging from adultery to a series of smaller offenses. So many people can recant every negative situation they went through in life but are challenged to remember the good ones. During our growing years most of us have changed physical addresses many, many times. But our hearts and minds have a tendency to stay stuck in events and situations at those same physical addresses for which we chosen not to let go. The bible gives us Jesus Christ as the highest aspiration to forgiveness. This verse makes known human frailties and reveals the struggles involved in growing to true spirit filled love, but nevertheless, it is a path worth staying on.

Okay. I Can Forgive, But How Do I Forget?

In Philippians 3:11-14 we are told by The Apostle Paul *"That if possible I may attain to the (spiritual and moral) resurrection [that lifts me] out from among the dead (even while in the body). Not that I have now attained (this ideal), or have already been made perfect, but I press on to lay hold of and make my own , that for which Christ Jesus has laid hold of me and made me His own. I do not consider, brethren, that I have captured and made it my own (yet): but one thing I do [It is my one aspiration]: forgetting what lies behind and straining forward to what lies ahead, I press on toward the goal to win the [supreme and heavenly] prize to which God in Christ Jesus is calling us upward."*

*"One cannot volunteer
their free will if it is held
captive by other passions."*

— *Charles Rivers*

Freeing Your Home of Addictions

There is but one thing in life standing between you and your ability to volunteer freely of your heart and that is whatever addictive behavior you hold nearer to your heart than your spouse. In Matthew 6:21 we are told, *"For where your treasure is, there your heart will be also."* So in order to grow into a closer bond we will discuss some of the root causes of addictive behavior and how to rid your home of them.

Some addictive triggering mechanisms — If what we do for a life beyond work does not ignite our passion for living then we will lean on artificial stimulants for that lost excitement. This is where drugs, alcohol, pornography and the like originate. When people replace their free time or their zest for life with career and responsibilities they open the door wide to all sorts of negative coping crutches known as addictions. Addictive habits have the tendency to initially feel like they help us cope with all sorts of things we refuse to face up to. Addictions are our way of dealing with the mundane stresses of life. But with each use of the addiction our threshold of things we have the ability to cope with becomes lowered. Besides that, addictions will ultimately take more from your life then they will ever add to it. They will alienate your love and family from you and change your view of the public and the public's view of you.

Men and women react differently under situations of boredom and stress. While not a hard and fast rule boredom may trigger some addictions in women, while stress is more of an addictive indicator in the lives of men. For others it may be a feeling of aloneness. But the trick is to finally take the time to be alone, feel that aloneness, bathe in that aloneness and attack that feeling. But remember when you need to turn to an addiction first track it back to whatever is either boring, stressing or making you lonely and deal with that first in a positive way. Men and women both exist within normal boundaries on our personal morale scale until we go through an internal or external crisis. Beyond this point we consciously choose to leave that morale scale to use addictions in hopes of centering ourselves. The addictive personality does not center his/herself in spiritual love but in his/her own balancing scales. The addictive person operates in their mind and with their own resources to deal with pain. In essence, we become physician and pharmacist in the management of pain and pleasure.

Some men and women both who procrastinate to a level of risk in their jobs, homes or personal lives may reach for whatever risky behavior will calm their uneasy feelings. When procrastination leads to stress and an addictive nature, this is usually our green light to act on that event or project we have been putting off. For some people that would mean working on a failing relationship or for others moving beyond a career that robs their soul. But the answer for most should be a calling to move closer to the spiritual love for the comfort we seek instead of addictions that act on the body and kill the spirit with each successive use.

"An addiction
is forever thwarted
once its captive begins to come to
grips with its causes instead
of managing its
symptoms."

— *Charles Rivers*

The Fastest Acting Addiction is Neither Ingested nor Inhaled

All humans are born with what will be their future sexuality. Now here is where we get in trouble. Everyone has that young friend who somehow magically finds a pornographic book that he/she wants to share with you. Others have those dirty little relatives that unintentionally leave us easy access to adult films and books. Now once you view these items with your eyes they go straight to your very soul. You are now hooked, but differently than any other addiction.

External Addictions Verses Internal Addictions — Of all of the addictions to have, I believe pornography is the worst. Here's why: most of the addictions we normally face have to be placed within our bodies before we can become addicted. Sure enough, we have the ability to receive lifelong addictions through any one of our five senses. But the worst addictive nature to take internally comes through the eyes, the lamp of the body. We are told in Luke 11:34-36 that, *"Your eye is the lamp of your body. When your eyes are good, your whole body also is full* *of light. But when they are bad, your body also is full of darkness. See to it, then, that the light within you is not darkness. Therefore, if your whole body is full of light, and no part of it dark, it will be completely lighted, as when the light of a lamp shines on you."*

If you were never addicted to anything and I placed three items in front of you — a pack of cigarettes, a bottle of beer and a pornographic magazine something wickedly controlling would reveal itself within your human consciousness.

Simply viewing the cigarettes on that table will never get you hooked on smoking them. You would have to inhale the smoke into your body before they would have any effect on the pleasure centers of your brain. Then you would have to get beyond the distaste and the gag effect (that comes with carcinogens) of many cigarettes before their addictive nature could ever take a hold and dominate your free will. Similarly, by viewing the beer you would not have the experience of drunkenness or alcoholic addiction . . . it must be ingested. The average person would have to drink many cans, depending on their threshold or tolerance of addiction to alcohol. Then you would have to get beyond its unpleasant taste and alcoholic sickness-es before the addiction formed to control your free will. But to open the pornographic magazine and visualize an eternal stimulus you know nothing of has the potential to get you hooked immediately on one page. It arouses your brains sexual centers and releases the addictive chemical dopamine, which makes you desire it even more. Like any other addiction, it will make you lie about the fact that you engage in it.

With pornography a person neither has to face the gag effect nor get beyond the distaste. The only aversion barrier to be defeated is our personal morale scale. Once you take in the pornographic material with the eyes, the brain becomes addicted bypassing that moral scale and your lamp becomes darkened.

From that day forward your views of the opposite gender become skewed in your eyes to fulfill a natural high. Your light upon viewing pornography will be permanently snuffed out. When it comes to viewing the opposite gender, one must now rely on the other four senses to understand true love. One is promised that their eyes will be opened at a young age after viewing pornography, but actually their eyes become closed to all other levels of love beyond the erotic.

A spouse who has relied upon pornography to darken their soul must now learn how to listen to his/her spouse. They must learn how to address their spouse with a hand touch that is other than to arouse oneself sexually. He/she must learn how to taste his spouse with non-sexual gentle kissing for that is what these pornographic stimuli lack. They should learn how to enjoy their spouse's smell outside of a completely sexual perfumed state of arousal. An addiction will steal what is left of your pride before taking its final hold of you. The nature of any addiction is that just before it entirely consumes the free will of its host it has them pass it on to another person suggestively as fun who is addiction-free. With porn unlike most addictive drugs, you don't inhale it, you don't inject it — you just view it.

*"Most people turn
to Erotic love because it
is one of the last loves they are sure to
feel in areas of life where human
touch becomes void of Philia
and Agape love."*

— *Charles Rivers*

Why the Strong Hold of Pornography and Extramarital Affairs?

In Matthew 12:29 we are asked this question: *"How can a person go into a strong man's house and carry off his goods without first binding the strong man? Then indeed he may plunder the house."* This biblical verse gives us the analogy of how even the strongest among us physically or spiritually can be bound by what we have as a weakness. The will to resist addictive behaviors must be hijacked before people can be bound and led in a destructive direction willfully.

No addiction has any control over our bodies without us first submitting our free will to it. In fact, once people escape addictions, they choose to take back the free will they allowed the addictive stimuli to control. Drugs have no hold over the body except that they have the key to sabotaging the body's own chemistry. In the brain the chemical dopamine, oxitosin and serotonin helps to regulate our moods and well being. The chemical dopamine helps to transmit nerve impulses within the brain between sending and receiving nerve receptors. Serotonin is widely distributed through the body and the brain and affects change on our emotional moods. Oxitosin, although a chemical released after a woman has birth In preparation for breast feeding also Is released during orgasm In both sexes. In the brain, oxitosin Is Involved In social recognition and bonding, and might be Involved In the formation of trust between people. This chemical stands to reason for mothers do develop a sense of oneness with their newborns and people who are in a committed sexual relationship develop a sense of oneness during the act of sexual intercourse.

Addictions such as cocaine and other stimuli driven addictions hijack the body's natural production of the chemical such as dopamine, thereby blocking its steady flow between neuron connectors. It blocks one side of the receiving connectors so that chemicals such as dopamine are able to build up heavily on one side of the neuron connector, raising it to a level of euphoria. In a sense we are not high on the drugs we take but on our own body's chemistry. The chemical dopamine is released at a proportionately higher rate during sex, equivalent to an intense drug high for just a brief moment during orgasm.

Dopamine is also released at a constantly higher rate while you're watching pornographic material than in your normal lovemaking. This is why no one should accept the advice of anyone who suggests that adult films will enhance your lovemaking. The only thing that will happen is that you will be hooked on the pornography and not a healthy sex life with your spouse. The same goes for marriages with people who are serial adulterers. They end up getting hooked on the dopamine high in the brain while participating in illicit sexual acts more than they do having sex with the person they are with.

When spiritual couples come to me with relationship problems, I often find a base influence has been infecting their sexual life as a couple. Either the husband or the wife that is supposed to be walking in the ways of love will profess that they are in the "dog house sexually." This is a terminology used when one spouse denies the other sexual erotic love to punish them for any number of perceived wrongs. It harkens back to a dog that may have done something damaging in the masters house and is then sent out to stay in their dog house separate from the warm conveniences of the main home. Either husband or wife may be taking up residence on the couch or in some other part of the house even though they should be sleeping together. In other odd circumstances they may share the same bed in a sexless relationship just as long as no one crosses the center line of the bed. Some of these same bed situations find both spouses sleeping so close to the opposite edge from each other they risk falling off the side in their sleep.

This conduct is most dangerous to the life of any committed relationship. It is dangerous because one spouse creates a glass ceiling for the other in one of the three areas of spiritual love. Usually when you do this in a society that is obsessed with Erotic (sexual) love someone will come along with a hammer to break that glass ceiling. Strange people beyond the borders of your home, who have the intention of committing adultery, target your spouse in this vulnerable state of sexually charged emotions.

But the reason all illicit relationships, pornography and fantasies fail to deliver true satisfied love over the long haul is that your concentration is never on the person you are engaging in a sexual relationship with but the arousal behind it. When you bring only your mind to bed you leave Philia (friendship) and Agape (true) love at the bedroom door. All you have left is an erotically exciting sexual experience, and this experience is not much different than bringing yourself to orgasm.

The sexual relationship becomes all about you having sex with yourself and your internal thoughts. This is love in the most non spiritual realm. For one to enjoy erotically stimulated fantasies love with their spouse in a room must think of another who is not present in that room. The act of sexual love should be with the person you are with and not in your head with pretended imaginations. Any type of addiction is meant to satisfy the selfish needs of the individual to escape pain for pleasure. Another person who has to exist as codependent in an addiction with you does not receive your pleasure. All the alcohol I can consume in the world will never make my wife drunk.

That is precisely why a physically erotic-type dating relationship is usually highest touted but shortest lived of any of the three loves. The relationship if not allowed to grow is mainly sex based and the person you are having sex with becomes a tool for our sexual gratification. They are never allowed to rise up to the level of a human, which starts at the Philia (friendship) level. Most sexually-based relationships refuse to go to this level because they fear this will kill the maximum pleasurable experience of the sexual relationship. It is best that both participants in this natural brain high remain neutral with their feelings and concerns in life in order to protect the great sexual feelings that are aroused by addictive highs.

What these relationships fail to appreciate is that sex becomes more intimate if you bring all three loves to bed with you. Eros (sexual) love is fine as a good inducer of the sexual act but it does not honor the openness of the Philia (friendship) love as in respect to the sexual act. Couples that have a good friendship relationship can communicate their sexual desires and sexual positions towards one another much more easily instead of patterning the sexual acts of adult films. Eros (sexual) love alone can never understand that couples who exist on an Agape (true) level of love would not want to commit adultery against their spouse. People who have truly achieved Agape (true) love understand that the people who they love should be respected as a creation of God and not as a created pleasure tool.

In coaching couples, I have been known to take away from them the tools of using sex as a weapon in the relationship in order to get what they want. For who could withhold *water* (a metaphor for sex) in a country that is satiated with faucets? In other words, you live in a society where not only will people want to commit adultery with your spouse but it bothers the heck out of them in some sick way to see them thirst for something that everyone freely offers.

The late Norman Vincent Peale once said, *"Change your thoughts and you change the world."* What Peale meant when he penned this statement many years past was that if you changed your thoughts of the world from negative to positive, your outlook on everything and everyone around you would follow suit. The physical world that used to frustrate you would not change, but you would — and that is half the battle most of us face in trying times.

Create More Sunny Days than Rainy

Difficult experiences in life have the tendency to bring out the worst in us and, for some of us, quite often depression. We lash out at those we love. This is why if any marriage is to be genuine and long lasting, it is impossible to be strong

119

and one in marriage under trying circumstances in an Eros (sexual) relationship. You must be at least a Philia (friendship) relationship, optimally an Agape (true) one. Spirit centered couples who are not friends in hard times usually fall apart over the incident and pull apart from one another. In troubled times, an "everyone for themselves" attitude will exist in these homes.

But these are the times when we should never bolt to decisions. Why, because between the flight or fight mentality that we all possess there is always room for pause. If you could do well under trying times as a single person, then with your spouse at your side things should be twice as nice. If the bad times that we all face bring out the blaming mechanism in you, then this is another reason to use the time to improve yourself. Remember we learn more about ourselves with someone of the opposite nature then we ever could in the presence of someone of like mind.

"The good times
in life are like pepper
sprinkled over a
plate of grits."

— Charles Rivers

Celebrating the Bad Times as Good

Not only have I always suggested this to couples but this is my motto and I use this exercise religiously. You may think its crazy, but it gets even wilder. When you go through life's most trying situations celebrate it just as you would life's up moments. Go to your grocer's pastry section and purchase a sheet cake with stenciling of whatever hurdle you are facing in life currently. For example, stenciling like "we are going through financial difficulties and we can only go up from here". What about putting the amount in dollars of the debt you currently owe to your creditors that are hounding you. By all means don't forget those blessed cake titles, "I just got fired."

Secondly, get either a bottle of non-alcoholic or regular champagne and commemorate the moment, for, with God, you won't be there long. If we don't celebrate the bad times in living as life's training aide, we are not celebrating life at all. For our existence entails the good, bad and uninteresting. If we live only to celebrate what you deem as the good times, they may become few and far in between. The good times in life are sometimes sprinkled between the lulls and trials. It makes it much easier to come back from a hit in life if you don't begrudge yourself going through it. In fact you will come to realize once life closes one door for you it opens a nicer one. If life had to close this door in your life it probably was because you did not do so yourself. If it opened a door for you in life it was because only you can enter that new existence.

I've given you the medicine to allow you to look back and laugh at the experience. Remember that you can never have any memorable occasions without film, so take plenty of

The Value of the Human Spirit

pictures. This is written poetically well in the Psalms 30:5, *"Weeping may endure for a night, but joy comes in the morning."* Now that you have come to grips with your problems as a couple and changed your outlook on the situation, prepare to receive increase. For the Lord your heavenly Father always rewards learning. So receive wholeheartedly the lesson in the down times and prepare for the success that will ultimately come during the good. Remembering that all of us in life will take financial hits at every level of financial prosperity. But know this, that you can make it through because your spirit is mightier than your net worth is on paper.

"If one's intrinsic value is based solely upon earnings potential, it is a safe bet to assume that his or her internal emotions will be guided by the up and downward ticks of their personal net worth."

— Charles Rivers

Evolve
into one
beautiful couple, for you
dared to risk your heart with
someone who was separate and distinct
from your will. You have successfully died to self
if you have strived in earnest to live God's
Agape love. Along the journey you
have become a more likeable,
loveable and easy to
live with human
being.

4

Surrendered

Baggage

*"For what
activates the best
in all of us does not reside
within any of us, but rest in those
we allow to influence
our soul."*

— *Charles Rivers*

If you ever want the best a relationship has you must open your heart to it fully. Even if you believe you have

The Evolution of the Human Spirit in Spirit

been hurt prior to the relationship or during it. Throughout history many people have asked what beauty could ever come from such cruel tragedies of the world we live in. My answer to that question is that there is much more to be learned and healed over trying times then there ever will be in the good times. Jesus Christ endured great suffering and pains as he bore each lash of the soldier's whip for all of the sins of mankind. Even under tremendous pains of being nailed to the cross, he could already see triumph for his followers through the tragedy of the moment. After the third day, he ascended to the right hand of his father in heaven and opened the door to salvation and the most beautiful religion that ever graced the face of this blue ball we call earth.

There are far too many stories and examples of people who have either turned their lives or other people's lives around because of pain or tragedy. I am reminded of just such an example that proves this type of evolution of the human spirit. It is the story of a little girl called Denise. Denise, as a young adult, was frequently overheard saying, *"I have no talent. What can I do in life?"* She had allowed a damaged past to color her opinion of her self worth and her importance to this world. Denise was born into poverty in the rural Southern portion of the state of Texas. By the age of six months, she was in the care of her cousins as foster parents. She was second to the youngest of six other siblings who had been forcibly removed from the care of her birth parents by the local authorities.

The local government would charge of the parents with abuse. Denise would never again come to live under the same roof with her natural parents. Eventually through quite a bit of structuring Denise did find a good foster home and had come to accept her new foster mother as a loving person. Unfortunately Denise's care giver died just as she was beginning to grow on her at the tender age of thirteen. This was devastating to the emotions of a girl who had never seen any sense of permanence in her still young life. Because of this her attitude about life took on a defensive posture, which is what one expects from a child who becomes skeptical of attachments to people who are transient in their lives.

Due to her foster mother's passing, she never really recovered her drive for excelling in school. By the age of seventeen years she became disenfranchised with the public school system and decided to drop out of high school. Within the next couple of years she would become disenchanted with the relationships she shared with the men she dated. In her own words she told me, "I thought that relationships were tiresome, boring and false." By the age nineteen years she decided to marry the man she believed she fell in love with. But it did not take long for the fallout of that painful type of upbringing to threaten the safety of her blossoming marriage. But her husband, knowing similar pains from his own upbringing, decided to stick it out with Denise for as long as it took for her to heal. There were many times when he just wanted to walk away but he knew you don't just abandon your spouse when they are hurting the worst. Their relationship became whole after her husband educated himself in the trials, pains and joys that were similar to all marriages.

That was almost ten years ago, and that young lady who was healed and saved is my wife. She has been the inspiration for all of the books that I have ever written on marriage and relationships. She is the reason that I committed to instructing couples in love at the seminars we hold. If not for her and my past tragedy, you would not be able to experience the triumph of healing your relationship through this book you are reading.

She had been mistaken many years ago when she believed

she had no gift to give to the world. Because God wanted us to partner together, great things have happened to heal both of our lives: past and present. Because of that little girl, my books are read by thousands of people each year who want to transition in earnest from marital pain to marital bliss. I believe there is a little Denise in every town all around the world who thinks of themselves just the way she did. Yes that small girl from that little Southern town has been God's greatest tool for relationship change that I have ever witnessed. I mean I saw every nuance of pain In my parents relationship reflected In mine. During the entire time I was single I witnessed many couples bicker argue and fight. But It was when I noticed that these were just the patterns that people have In relationships and not the relationship that I saw an avenue for change In a permanent way.

For I have learned that what was best in me did not reside in me, but lived in her most secretive unhealed areas. Most likely you can locate similar situations in someone you know or even under your own roof.

Keep Your Heart Open to Change

As loving couples we must try to learn from one another instead of just teaching and preaching. For if two people are to successfully communicate it will have to exist on a two way street. When we talk at our spouse, this is known as dictating and not communication. Communication is the exchange of information or ideas. But often we get stuck in an immature rut of toning out one another unless it serves our greater good.

If we don't allow input in from a shared coupling then there can be no relationship. It only falls apart from the weight of its own indifference. At this point, if the couple does not rectify the situation, they will both seek relationships outside of the home. It may be from the opposite gender for sex or the same gender for friendship. Because all of us, at sometime in our lives, need someone to communicate with. That is why most people talk their friends' ears off — because they cannot communicate effectively with their own spouse.

*"A person will
sabotage their individual
happiness when they cease
to feel importance in
their daily life."*

— Charles Rivers

A married man who cannot communicate with his wife finds his way into topless nightclubs where women reveal their bodies while people who don't like themselves or their spouses much look on. A wife who finds herself in the same loveless relationship discovers that she has grown a fondness for a coworker who sees her as her husband once did.

Her coworker will find no problem with acting on the opportunity to ensnare a wife who is in pain for his own erotic gratification. When we engage in these relationships we don't move forward but backwards into the realm of the Erotic (sexual) love. Why do people neglect to tell the truth in relationships? It is because they either know or have a feeling that the person they are in a relationship with will walk out on them. I taught you earlier that real love will seek to kill false love in a relationship wherever it exists. But if one can not speak the truth in love they exist in a phony relationship that is built on lies and untruths.

One should never have to fear that the person you love the most will abandon you if you tell them the truth or where you are hurting. That is precisely why love is called to a higher plateau than merely erotic love. For it is only at the highest levels of consciousness that someone can be understood for most secretive areas or their dirtiest little secrets.

"When you're green you're growing,
and when you stop you start to rot."

— Ray Krok

Mr. Krok, the founder of the McDonalds restaurant corporation, was right when he made this true statement concerning business. He gave us the analogy of any plant that grows from seed to bloom has a green life cycle until its preset maturity date. Then the plant starts to slowly die and then to rot. We can also make this comparison to relationships that start out on fire only to end with a fizzle. In marriage, you have to come up with just as many ideas as you would lend your business to make it extremely successful.

There is not a business in the world that if successful did not gage where they were that moment and learn how they could be more profitable and productive in the upcoming year. Some relationships are fast growing weeds and others are slow growing oaks. In the marriage relationship the Lord gives us a lot of small instances in which to practice being receptive to our spouse's input. The point we refuse to grow with our spouse will be remembered as our relationship's maturation date, followed shortly by its die back date. Without this openness we can not grow together. For we were designed to grow side by side as one flesh and not by one knowing or withholding from the other.

It is the better decision made by two instead of one. It is better to live as two instead of one. In Ecclesiastes 4:8-11 we are told, *"Here is one alone — no one with him; he neither has child nor brother. Yet there is no end to all his labor, neither does he ask, for whom do I labor and deprive myself good? This is also vanity (emptiness, falsity, and futility); yes, it is a painful effort and an unhappy business. Two are better than one, because they have a good (more satisfying) reward for their labor; For if they fall, the one will lift up his fellow, But woe to him who is alone when he falls and has not another to lift him up! Again, if two lie down together, then they have warmth; but how can one be warm alone?"*

Why the Agreement of Two Over the One?

"Any house divided against itself
shall not stand."

— Matthew 12:25

God Intended Marriage to be the World's Most Powerful Team

We are given many chances to merge opinions and decisions as a practice to draw us nearer to one another. As a treasure and consequence of each agreed upon decision, we are drawn closer to God. Each disagreement and argument draws us ever closer to the demonic realm and destruction. We are not to fight with one another but to find agreement from conflict. To paraphrase what Dr. Robert H. Schuller once said "*The best thing that one can do is to change a collision into a coalition.*" Have you ever seen any member of a professional football team tackle one of his own players during a game? Teamwork is the basis for all intimate relationships. In our mutual struggle we become bonded with one another towards our goals.

Sure you will have differences of opinions as all people do. But that is what will make your team successful. In life one spouse prefers to go to a fast food restaurant while the other wants to go to a finer restaurant. One likes canned green beans and the other can't stand them. She parks in the driveway while he prefers the street. These small times of flexibility are merely child's play for the larger decisions that lie ahead.

So if you notice a problem in your relationship with unspoken signals, don't wait for the emergency — move with a sense of urgency. Sometimes our human spirit can get so wounded that we won't be able to open up to those closest to us. I see this all the time from couples who fail to recognize non-verbal cues from their spouse that their friends can see from half a mile away. Usually in defense of their actions, a husband or wife will tell me that their spouse should tell them what is wrong. "Do they expect me to be a mind reader?" I am asked. I would settle for this excuse if they had not been so well attuned to reading their out of the home best friend's thoughts.

"For one can never really give
away a love they are too
frightened to possess
themselves.

— Charles Rivers

"Keith is so lazy he doesn't even help me change his own daughter's diapers," was the condemnation Tammy levied against her husband. Keith and Tammy were the last to visit me before what was supposed

How Easily are Signals Misread

to be a long enjoyable weekend at a late night relationship session. Often times couples who come to me are total strangers to marital assistance and lose their ability to speak shortly after sitting down. The next thing they do is usually blame one another with every fiber of their being. But I like to set the tone of the meeting by opening up to the true problems of the relationship instead of going around in circles over issues that have nothing to do with anything.

I accomplish this by choosing the spouse who is less boisterous to speak shortly after calming down the louder one. So once I got Tammy calm enough, I told her, that Keith, her husband, was going to tell her something that he has never told her before in his life. I do this because I have discovered that no matter what level of growth a marriage is in, spouses hold painful secrets closest to their heart if the other spouse is not open to unblemished intimacy. Tammy sat there with an attitude of believing she knew all there was to know about Keith. She believed if anything I didn't know him or have a clue about their relationship. He looked at me hesitantly at first then turned to her all at once and blurted out the unvarnished truth. Keith in a shaky voice said "I was molested as a child by my Aunt and my sisters on varying occasions as a child."

This childhood trauma was very emasculating for Keith at an age when his sexuality was yet to be formed. This hap-

133

pening in Keith's life gave clear justification as to why, in his mind, he was avoiding changing his own daughter's diapers. It was not due to him being lazy in parenting but he thought if he could avoid close contact with his daughter in intimate places she would be safe from what happened to him as a child. For so many years Keith had truly thought that whatever was pressed down upon him became him and was just waiting to get out demonstratively. I tell you that couple grew closer that afternoon than they ever did over the previous nine years of marriage. Today Keith shares the concerns of his spirit with God and his wife instead of trying to bear them on his own.

For you see, the only danger his daughter was in was having a father that was growing more and more distant with his love. Since he had never been given any true Agape (true) love at home, he could only offer Erotic love until he became healed. If that daughter of his had gotten any older she would have believed her daddy hated her by the distance he kept from her. Also, since he would have been unavailable for love, the doors would be left wide open for young boys to bring pretentious love to her in the same form of Erotic (sexual love) the dad was trying to avoid. Often times what we run from and fear most in life becomes ever so attractive to our existence.

> *"What brought*
> *You through the last ten*
> *years of your life won't carry*
> *you the next ten."*
>
> — *John Young Phelps*

As we come ever closer to the end of this book on relationship renewal I want you to remember that for every dead end your relationship faces you are being called up to a higher level of love. If you want to truly call down the awesome power

Be in Relationship One to Another

of the God of this universe then you must learn the properties of the mightiest word in the Jewish Torah. The word *Devekut*, pronounced *Day·vay·koot* is interpreted in the English language as *Cleave*. In the book *Domestic Baggage*, I explained to you the meaning of cleave but we must view its definition as a lifestyle.

There are only two instances in which this word is spoken in relationship between the closeness of two separate entities. If you are reading this book right now you are in the most powerful company. For God the Father shares his style of sacred relationship with man only through its meaning. The first time the word cleave is ever used in the presence of mankind is in the Garden of Eden in relation to the marriage of Adam and Eve.

The second time it is mentioned in faithful covenant relationship is between almighty God and those who wish to remain closest to him. In Deuteronomy 11:22 God tells us, *"That for if you diligently keep all this commandment which I command you to do, to love the Lord your God, to walk in all His ways, and to cleave to Him."* Then God says he will give you the desires of your heart. Now is that not the same ingredient to getting the desires of your heart in marriage?

When we fail to do this properly, we get ourselves in trouble. Many of us go to spiritual gatherings and try to cleave to God in our own way while not cleaving successfully to our spouses in the custom they are due. The Creator shows us that we should cleave in both relationships in order to find out what real love is. When we strive to love God while failing to get along with our spouses we mock the teachings of the Father and His Son. So we must be in relationship with our spouse as we are to God or we pay lip service of our love to both and as a consequence end up not being respected by either.

Understanding the Gifts of Corrective Criticism

In Genesis we are told that God made man and woman in His own image. But what does that really mean, people ask? Is God a man or a woman or both? God is both, but not in the sense of our earthly bodies. Throughout the bible you will note that God Is represented as being a God of *justice* and at times a God of *mercy*. When the children of God were living outside of the laws of love they called condemnation down upon themselves and His justice. But you will find just as many occasions that people lived within the laws of love and were rewarded mercifully. Then at other times without cause or just purpose God extended his mercy to His people that did not either expect or deserve It.

This Is why when It says that God made man and woman In his own Image It was of the nature of love; justice and mercy. The male animal of the human species represents the mirrored Image of Gods justice. While the female animal is best represented by God's mercy on earth. That Is why you will find It hard to agree In an argument If you just see the world based upon your genders point of view. It is when you combine the strengths of both that you get a truer picture of what two halves bring to the experience of whole. Disagreements within a marriage represent the checks and balances that the Father placed to bring all relationship to a consensus or all false love relationships to true love or dissolution.

Learning the Art of Communion

You can only give positive reflections of your spouse's conscious thoughts if you are in constant relationship to them. Webster's defines the word "relationship" as *a connection, association or involvement, a connection between persons by blood or marriage; kinship*. So if we desire the gift of reciprocal love from God and our spouse we must be in constant relationship in order to cleave. The second greatest thing in cleaving in love is that no matter if you are sick, rich or poor, whatever may come your way, true love will be there by your side.

Throughout the New Testament you will find many Instances in which Jesus associated with his disciples or strangers by fellowshipping. The act of fellowshipping means to befriend another and in the case of Christ that meant to spread the gospel to whomever he came in contact with. But what I find greatest about Christ ability to connect with others is that it was done most often times over a meal. That is the best time to get acquainted with the ones you love face to face over the breaking of bread. He practiced this habit throughout his entire ministry and even after his resurrection with his disciples on the shores of the Tiberias Sea.

In Hebrews 13:5 says that, *"He (God) Himself has said I will not in any way fail you nor give up nor leave you without support. I will not, I will not, I will not in any degree leave you helpless nor forsake nor let you down."* Now wouldn't it be absolutely fantastic, as husbands and wives, if we could treat our spouses to the same love that God treats us to? We should never forsake our spouses since we are governed by the same principles of cleaving relationships.

> *"Life is a process*
> *of discovering oneself. Once*
> *found you are truly lost*
> *and God is at work*
> *through you."*
>
> — *Charles Rivers*

Completing Love's Full Circle

A child is born with a form of Agape (true) love and before that child dies it will have lost but hopefully rediscovered that (Agape) love to make it to the kingdom of heaven. This is why Jesus Christ proclaimed in Matthew 18:3, *"No one will make it to the kingdom of heaven until they first become as little children again."*

It was as infants that we loved all people regardless of gender, race or backgrounds. It was as a child that we shared for the sake of sharing even with strangers. It was as a child that we forgave merely for the sake of forgiveness. Then towards our weaning youth we slowly transition away from Agape love towards Philia love for the people we call our friends. In this stage of life we take on a form of prejudice of not liking people who are not in our group or who don't think as we do. In this stage of our lives, sharing and forgiveness becomes limited to our personal friends only.

Beyond our preteen years, if we are not careful, we transition to the lowest stage of love for the opposite gender. Oddly enough, though our attractions for the opposite gender are the highest they will ever be at this point, our respect for them personally may be the lowest. We may have avoided them our entire young lives but now we are raging with hormones that prepare our bodies for procreation. By this time we are either estranged from true love or trying to find love in the rush, rush of everyday life. Finding our way back to love will be made easier as a loving person then it ever will be an embittered one.

The relationship of love allows us to transition gradually back up that ladder of love with someone instead of by ourselves. After the wedding we are joined in an Eros love relationship, but we can move to a Philia love with our spouse on our return path back to our estranged relationship to God and Agape (true) love. That is why the longest road any one of us will ever take in life is back to finding God's love and ourselves.

Most of our arguments in marriage occur when we are in an Eros relationship with one another — no matter how long we've been acquainted. Some spiritual couples carry secular gender wars that should stay beyond their door right into the love of their sanctified homes.

But competition between two loving Individuals robs both of closeness and financial support that only a couple could provide for one another. A wife who works and becomes pregnant should be able to count on her husband when she has to take a sabbatical from her career. You cannot count on this type of financial support from an outside of the home friend. Sure a friend can loan you money and support when you are in a pinch, but can they do it without complaint everyday for the rest of your life?

A husband who is injured and bed bound for a time should be able to count on his wife's income to see him through to wellness. But would you be able to get a friend to do that beyond the limits of their time or financial capability? When we compete with our spouse it makes about as much sense as two people rowing in a canoe in opposite directions while still expecting to go forward. To do this would cause the canoe to remain in place, spinning in circles. So take the time to know each other beyond the surface. The bible tells us in Mark 12:25 that, *"For when they shall rise from the dead, they neither marry, nor are given in marriage; but are as the angels which are in heaven."* So our earthly relationships represent the only time we will share this type of exclusivity love with one another.

Use each and every day to work towards Agape love and to cleave to your spouse. Nowhere in the bible does it suggest that we should cleave to our outside of the home friends or jobs, but we do. In fact we will even let our families go and fight for our friends and jobs. Most families in the technological age can easily service between six hundred to one thousand people a day effectively through our communities schools and jobs. Simultaneously, this same family could fail at servicing just the handful of people that reside within the walls of their shared homes.

"Many parents see their children's wants as needs and their spouse's needs as wants."

— *Charles Rivers*

Amy sat quietly seething with her arms folded and teeth clinched in a defensive posture at a session between her and her husband. But she was not alone, for there were several things in their relationship that also dis-

If You Love the Husband, He Will Love the Child

turbed her husband about Amy. Chief on Amy's list of grievances was that her husband never spent as much time with the children as she thought a father should. After listening intently to the complaints from both sides I concluded that Amy although correct in her assumption had put her love to her husband, who preceded her beautiful children, on the back burner for many years. Amy had made herself ready to dedicate the rest of her life to her children while at the same time being most unconcerned to her husband. Sure enough, men should participate in the lives of their children: especially in ways other than being a provider and a disciplinarian. But there is a dilemma in a negative coupling the way men and women view the role of father.

Males do not go through the birthing process; they don't go through a single ounce of internal growing pains of a new embryo. But most of all they don't possess the desire that predates adolescence, as women do, to have children. But what men are great at is being overly defensive and guarding of their relationship with their wives if they must share her with anyone else. So wives, if this is your dilemma at home, let me enlighten you what to do to turn the situation around. First, do not pull away from your spouse during pregnancy and especially after delivery. For most adulterous affairs are committed by the husbands of pregnant wives in the first and final trimester of pregnancy.

Why? Because the husband feels alone in the presence of their wives. He begins to feel the love you once directed towards him shift to another person. A pregnant woman naturally draws her focus inward or towards her friends for support during these critical stages of pregnancy. To the male, an outside observer, the relationship becomes more about the mother and baby and less about the person who helped to create the new wonder. To bring this husband into the fold all you have to do is show him strong Agape (true) love. Not all but from my observations some men develop a disconnection after labor with their child if the mother disconnects with the father during pregnancy.

So if your love for your husband is not any different than it is for his child, he will love that child. Why, because men see their own small children as an extension of the mother existence long before they will ever truly begin to see them as their children on a fatherly level. So if you either Ignore or feel Indifferent toward the father he will more than likely Ignore or feel Indifferent toward his child. Remember, love was never meant to be part and parceled out one way for the father and another for the child but people treated the same in Agape (true) love. Now, later on down the road, this father will grow to his rightful position of love for his child and participate freely without prompting. But for this man to arrive where he must with his children, he will need your help.

Amy understood this during our session when out of the blue she said, "I see what you're saying, I have been selfish with my love for my children, while at the same time missing what my husband had been lacking." To her husband she replied, "I had massaged our children's feet who were only two years old but I had never massaged your feet and for years I had ignored the pain in yours." This couple is now on the right road, and they are going to make it with loves help. Once his wife put her focus back on the relationship her husband put his focus back on his children and his wife. That father with a renewed love on his wife's part spends so much time now with his children his wife actually gets a break from doing it all herself.

"*Love is ever ready to believe the best of every person, its hopes are fadeless under all circumstances, and it endures everything without weakening. Love never fails or becomes obsolete or comes to an end.*"

1 Corinthians 13:7–8

It is a safe bet to say that by the time our children attend the first grade a part of their character are already set in cement. As parents, we must avoid the temptation to paint them with the same brush that society uses on them. If your

Every Child is an Individual Creation

child is a boy, you could fear him getting in trouble, hanging around with the wrong influences. If we have a daughter we could fear other children offering her drugs, her getting pregnant, or something worse. Most parents have these fears long before their children even reach school age.

When we do this we send our children the message: I expect the worst of you. It is shortly after this that we find ourselves not let down by their behaviors. Replace this outlook with a positive one in the future. We cannot be believers in true love while being disbelievers in his most precious of creations. To view our children as an outcome instead of a person is contradictory to the way we wish the world to see us.

None of us can stand to be lumped in a group that is not our choosing, especially a negative one. The late Bishop Fulton Sheen explained why you don't want to place labels on children. He tells a true story how he was sitting in a posh New York restaurant when he noticed a boy in a dirty T-shirt. The boy was occupied with swinging on the long plush drapes that lined the entrance into the restaurant. The maître d', noticing this, chased the little boy out of the restaurant and told him to never come back. The Bishop followed the distraught boy outside and asked him what his name was. Once the boy told the Bishop his name, the Bishop said it was a beautiful Irish name.

"You should be in Catholic school," the Bishop replied. The

145

boy responded, "I go to public school. I used to go to Catholic school but I got kicked out." The Bishop assured the boy that he would get him back in, despite the fact that the boy's mother had tried several times to get him reinstated.

The next day, the Bishop went down to that school and met with the principal and the Mother Superior. He inquired why they had kicked the young man out. The principal and the Mother Superior reiterated what the boy said. "He cannot come back here; his attitude is not accepted here." Hearing this, Bishop Sheen said, "Let me tell you a story about three boys who were kicked out of religious schools. The first boy was kicked out because he drew pictures while the class was going on. The second because he got in a series of skirmishes with other children, and the last because he had subversive pamphlets under his mattress."

The Bishop said, "Now no one knows who the valedictorian of any of their classes was but I'm sure that you are familiar with the three boys. The first was Hitler; the second was Stalin, and the last, Mussolini." The principal and the Mother Superior were shocked and let the boy back in school. The Bishop finished his story by telling us that the boy who was let back in school is now a missionary in Alaska. Surely what we look for in children or adults is what we will find. In Ephesians 6:4 it instructs parents, *"Fathers, do not irritate and provoke your children to anger (do not exasperate them to resentment), but rear them (tenderly) in the training and discipline and the counsel and admonition of the Lord."*

*"We discipline
our children for the very
same behaviors we excuse
ourselves of on a
daily basis."*

As a spiritual family you will live amongst a swirling barrage of opinions on the subject of discipline and your children. But remember if you can stick to the Agape (true love) principals for discipline you can never go wrong with your little ones and yourself. Many people who were raised either the wrong way or in an abusive situation become either paralyzed to stop their children or paralyze their children by stopping everything they do.

When to Correct and When to Instruct

Throughout the entire bible you will notice that God admonishes and praises in equal measure. His correction was for those out of his will or those living out of the principles of love. His praises were for those operating in the laws of love. Only death and destruction came from hate while life and relationship building came from true love. God's will is effectively keeping us in balance, protecting our very lives.

I sat with a father who still threatened his oldest son at age fifteen with whooping him. He had three other sons of younger ages that he screamed at to get them to do right. This father believed himself to be firmly in control of his children. But when you have to scream and carry on with strong discipline three years before your child goes into the world, you're the only person who lacks control. I made clear to the father that a whooping simply for the sake of discipline yields only immediate compliance.

If you spank a child who has not done his homework on a daily basis and is failing in school, you may see short term improvement. But soon enough, over time, those grades will drop off again until you have to lean on the spankings to maintain that grade point average. Another reason whooping alone doesn't work is because by itself it does not yield any lesson beyond getting whooped. Case in point, your child gets in a fight with a bigger child at school.

The older child is able to whoop your child in the playground conflict. Where is the lesson learned? The similarity to the whooping we gave is present. So when you spank your child and you only notice a pattern of immediate compliance, then change your approach. Raising little ones like this will turn them into adults who tell lies. As parents, we are presented with many occasions for giving our children life lessons.

Tell your children the right thing to do even when you don't think they are listening. Even during the times that they appear to be staring into space. Their rebellious brains are absorbing those critical messages better than their little butts ever will a whooping on these occasions. If you don't believe me and you are now a parent yourself, look back at your own history. Think on the occasions where your grandparents or parents tried to impart lifelong messages in your brain before or after you did something wrong.

Now fast forward to today and see if you can recall most if not all of what they were trying to impart upon your life. Look at how those warnings and instructions prevented you from great harm. Look at how they helped to shape the career path you chose. You may have stared into space back then or murmured under your breath in secret, as all young people will do, but the message did stick. I have spoken to adults who have lost their parents at an old age and they still can recant messages that were imparted to them from fifty years ago.

So if you must spank your child, use these guidelines. Spank the child when you are first not in a state of offense or irritated. Occasions for being offended present themselves after a long day's work, or from behavior that is naturally childlike in nature. Our child must have done something worthy of it and you have to be in the right frame of mind to carry it out without making it personal. Remembering that you are not spanking your children but sending down a legacy of discipline to generations to follow through this one child.

All children start out primarily honest, as sent by God from above. Although they do learn how to manipulate to get what they want, the true sense of lying does not manifest until they get in trouble for the first time. No matter if you are an infant or an elderly person, all humans have a tendency to lie when they are not proud of something they have done. Children learn to be creative at lying to avoid spankings or punishment.

Child Honesty Verses the Shameful Factor

Look at every situation in the bible where God was about to bring discipline on someone for an offense. What did each person that knew discipline was coming in advance do? They either lied or made up an excuse to cover their transgression. So if you pick up a pattern of lies in your little one you may need to change your form of discipline. This is so that you don't teach them to lie more than you teach them to obey what is right. Finally your children will be fine with discipline if you only take just as much time to praise their positive behavior as you do to catch them doing something wrong.

It is our humble mission as parents to put the best in our

children true love has to offer. We should never try to predict their future any more than we can predict our own. This is why we are instructed in Proverbs 22:6, *"Train up a child as you would have him go and when older he will never depart from it."*

This biblical passage recognizes that the child's free will as an adult can have him doing many things that will take him off of the narrow path to heaven and to the broad path to hell. But at the same time, it expects that they will return as long as the child within the adult has been rooted in love. Another bible passage that recognizes this is the Prodigal Son. In Luke 15:10 it states, *"Even so, I tell you, there is joy among and in the presence of angels of God over one (especially) wicked person who repents."* So even after doing your absolute best and having your child go astray, trust in God and pray for their faithful return as the Prodigal Son.

*"Conceive
in your minds eye
your child as being unique
and you will be a witness to
unique behaviors."*

— Charles Rivers

Your little one was born for a time such as now, not for a time such as you grew up in. This is my advice to parents who want to prepare their children for the future. So when we affect warnings on their conscious, we have to ensure that they are not based solely upon the pains we went through, otherwise our children will be ill prepared for what life reveals to them.

Because your child is unique, the most difficult balancing act you will ever perform is to stop trying to heal your personal past through them. If you bring to bear the full weight of your pains or pleasures upon your children's individual existence, they will spend the rest of their adult life trying to shake it off. Trust me; I have sat in on too many sessions where the biggest concern of the adult is how they can start living their dreams instead of their parent's nightmare. It is not incumbent upon any of us to relive our parent's upbringing, especially if it was bad. God the Father presents this same logic throughout the bible. Did you know that God never sent anyone through the same experience twice?

Some parents, molested in their youth, come to assume that children will be done the same unless we watch and restrict them harshly. Some adults faced poverty as children and fight for money at all costs. Others had too much money as children and they can recall no love to show that was equivalent to the value of that money. As adults these parents smother their children so they won't feel without love as they once did for the sake of money. But dealing with your little one this way is the same as discipline. Ensure that your advice or guidance is about the child and not about you.

Parents are more than providers to children; we are teachers to them. In fact, the longest school term anyone ever attended was not public or private but our home schooling. That's right: eighteen years of your life was spent in the classroom of your parents.

The classes we attended were familiar subjects like accounting, human relations and psychology to name a few. Sometimes, just like the real schools we attended, we weren't too fond of the teachers. Some teacher's behavior served little more than to push us in the opposite direction of our full potential. But just as with real schools, the teachers (parents) who see the best in us — even though we served up the worst — helped to shape and mold us for the future.

"But the fruit
of the Spirit is love, joy,
peace, patience, kindness,
goodness, faithfulness,
gentleness and
self control."

— *Galatians 5:22-23*

The Teacher Must Learn From the Pupil in Order to be Effective

Each child is as individual as the home they are born into — with maybe one exception. Children bring light to where the glow of youth in the parents has faded. We have much to teach our little ones by the age of eighteen, and much more to learn from them by age five. Your child will reveal through their nature, the humanity you lost in the process of becoming an adult. By the time the average couple decides to have children, they would have set their home up nicely where it is comfortable for adults. Parents will subsequently prepare a room wonderfully for a baby prior to its arrival.

But babies have no concept of boundaries between rooms or limits of other people's personal property. A toddler will throw up half a bottle of milk on your new expensive furniture along with your new clothing. That expensive crystal you bought prior to children becomes an attractive toy in their eyes, so you better place it up high if you want to keep it.

A toddler giggles simply because they enjoy the moment they are in, but an adult needs the stimulus of alcohol, drugs, or the like to loosen up and find a smile. Little ones are not like this any more than you were as a toddler. As a child you did not need drugs, legal or otherwise, to bring you up or down. You did not need caffeine to make it through the workday. Nor did you need alcohol to help you forget the week come Friday's celebration.

In the bible, it is written in 1 Corinthians 13:11 that, *"When I was a child I spoke as a child, I reasoned as a child but now that I am an adult I put away childish things."* But what that passage does not say is I put away my humanity in order to become an adult. I believe lost humanity, love for all, and compassion are the only things separating us from children. But Jesus said unless we become as children again (at heart) we will never see the kingdom of heaven. As adults we have a tendency to prematurely age the life out of our children's childhood in the same way it was done to us.

We go from admiring the newborn's birth to planning what college our child is going to and the ways he or she can compete effectively with their classmates. We falsely believe they need to act seriously as early as infancy for the world to take them that way. It is the behavioral equivalent to *Invasion of the Body Snatchers*. This movie's premise was that alien invaders used pods to replicate each human that they came in contact with in order to take their place in the world. The only thing the aliens could not replicate was the person's individual humanity and ability to have natural fun.

So once the person was converted they appeared to be nothing more than a robot without feelings. It was the job of those who had already been converted to seek out and reveal those who had not . I remember vividly, towards the end, a character telling another, "I went to sleep and it didn't hurt me. You should go to sleep." The only way to convert someone was in their sleep, so when they awoke they would be different. This is exactly what we do when we encourage our children to put their humanity to sleep and become the walking dead.

*"Children will
let you know when
you have concentrated on
yourself long enough."*

— Charles Rivers

All Children Have Built-In Mercury-Driven Temperaments

If your children cannot get your positive attention, they will ultimately settle for your negative attention. If you cannot give them the time of day for their concerns, they will act out to bring your attention to them. You see, children are the regulators or thermometers of every marriage. When a husband and wife go at one another, arguing and not getting along, it affects the children. No indifference in the home is just between the parents—it affects the home as a whole. If you have a school-aged child during home conflicts, you will see their grades dropping and their homework going undone.

Shortly thereafter you will begin to receive notes and telephone calls from their teacher about the child's work performance and attitude. The teacher will call mainly to prevent your child from failing; she will not be aware of your personal problems. But usually intervention from outside sources is enough to break the concentration between two warring adults, so as husband and wife we cease our strife and turn our attention towards our child to prevent them from failing. Over time, sure enough, the child's grades begin to climb and school behavior improves.

A great thing has just occurred courtesy of the Creator of the universe. God the Father placed a relationship regulator in children that they don't even know they possess. That is why children are successful at getting you to turn your attention and anger off of each other and back towards pressing needs. Additionally, the child has shown you as a team there is nothing that you cannot accomplish if you use your positive mind as well as the negative.

Have you noticed spikes or drops in your children's grades? If so, find out where your relationship was at least ten days prior to that event. If you can bring your behavior in line with Agape love you can not only regulate your child's achievement but you can have all of the love you have ever dreamed of in a family.

From the day they are born, children are like tape recorders with a human body. They watch everything we do and they listen to everything we say. During their childhood the record button is always stuck in the on position.

Children Are Like Little Camcorders

But once they reach adult life they hit the playback button

155

for their own personal lives. What is played back is what we allowed them to record of our behaviors, both positive and negative.

Now here is where things tend to get very difficult. If from your experience with them they cannot face life, they will hit the pause button and remain in place for as long as it takes them to go forward in the play mode. Unproductive years at a time will fly by in this mode. Pause in the lives of humans is usually a time for personal reflection on the past. It is equivalent to staring into a mirror or a calm pond. What happens when we stare at our image for a long time? The backdrop tends to fade away. People around us become invisible and so does what's really is important in life. We must pull back and allow the rest of life to come in.

Once most people have taught themselves to get beyond the pause, they will hit fast forward in an attempt to catch up to their life. Most people who find the fast forward button have learned to do so mainly because of forgiveness for their past. They have finally come to understand what role their parents played and that their parents did not mean any harm. If a person hits a brick wall with forgiveness they will hit the rewind button to go back and try to understand what happened. If what they recorded was beautiful, they can use it to enhance the present. If not, then God, psychiatry and self-help books will be leaned upon to help them hit the stop button on self-condemnation for something they had no control over. What most people need in that situation is to press eject on a non-Christian upbringing.

*"You will never
know what you might
have received if you are not
willing to give up what
you already have."*

— *Robert H. Schuller*

Each milestone we attain as a couple draws our family closer together, closer to God. Each milestone you achieve independent of one another's advice shows proof of your unwillingness to cleave. Along the way, through your entire relationship, you will come upon pressures when you refuse to bend to change that will help the relationship get over your old destructive ways . It is twice as important to our children as is to us to witness our peaceful agreements as we seek to merge different personalities.

Teaching Your Children the Values of Love

The secret ingredient to merging two different backgrounds is to let them go. As a couple you are building a new home together, as I said before, and not rebuilding your childhood home. As humans we see change as loss but to be successful in any long term relationship you will need to see change as gain. The lesson your child will take away from your love interactions is selfishness ends when you enter into a loving relationship.

Once you join with someone else in marriage you are not actually entering an Eros relationship but an Agape love

157

that slowly manifests itself far beyond the flash-in-the-pan sexual love affair. Expect to lose a lot of self on the way to finding yourselves as a couple. Prepare to gain more than you would have if you were trying to hold on to what you lost. If one is to win at love, he or she must first be willing to lose at it well.

"God is love,
and he who dwells and
continues in love dwells and
continues in God, and God
dwells and continues
in him."

— 1 John 4:16